Jesus Gathers Us Together

Early Childhood Leader Guide

Activities for children ages 3–5 who have not attended kindergarten

Copyright © 2016 Concordia Publishing House
3558 S. Jefferson Ave., St. Louis, MO 63118-3968
1-800-325-3040 · www.cph.org

Scripture quotations are from the ESV Bible® (The Holy Bible, English Standard Version®), copyright © 2001 by Crossway Bibles, a publishing ministry of Good News Publishers. Used by permission. All rights reserved.

The trade names and trademarks contained herein are the property of respective owners.

Manufactured in the United States of America

You can contact the Vacation Bible School team at Concordia Publishing House by email at vbsteam@cph.org.

Contents

Welcome to *Barnyard Roundup*   4

Course Chart   6

Site Highlights   8

What You Need (Resources and Supply List)   10

Advance Preparation for *Barnyard Roundup*   12

Make VBS Work for You and Your Kids! (VBS Options)   13

Lesson 1:   Jesus Is the Good Shepherd   14
John 10:1–18

Lesson 2:   Jesus Feeds 5,000 People   26
Mark 6:30–44; John 6:1–14

Lesson 3:   Jesus Tells about a Sower   38
Matthew 13:1–23

Lesson 4:   Jesus Tells about a Lost Son   50
Luke 15:11–32

Lesson 5:   Jesus Appears to Mary in the Garden   61
John 20:1–18

Welcome to *Barnyard Roundup!*

VBS 2016 is "farm-tastic!" In *Barnyard Roundup* VBS, young children will learn actively and through experiences designed just for them!

Your children will explore five Bible accounts that show how Jesus graciously gathers us together to be with Him with His abundant provision and saving protection, now and forever.

Kids and VBS Leaders will explore these concepts and the well-loved words of Psalm 23.

Key Theme
Jesus gathers us together.

Early Childhood Teams

Assign the early childhood children into Early Childhood Teams of five children and a Team Leader.

To organize your early childhood children, choose the best option for your setting.

Using Option 1, you'll divide the Early Childhood Teams into three Rotation Groups.

Using Option 2, you'll divide the Early Childhood Teams into six Rotation Groups.

If you have only one group of early childhood children, keep everyone together in one space for all activities. Set up the in-room rotations in small groups or do each activity with the whole group.

Whichever option you choose, pray that God empowers you to share all the great things Jesus does for His precious children!

Option 1: Three Rotation Sites

- **Arrival:** The children do a brief activity with the grown-ups who brought them. Then they play in thematic Learning Areas as others arrive.
- **Opening:** All early childhood classes gather in one location for their own Opening.
- **Bible story:** Children move back to classrooms for the Bible Story.

- **Rotations:** The children are organized into small groups within their classroom for three in-room rotations: Bible Story Application, Bible Challenge, and Crafts.
- **Snacks and games:** Small groups rejoin others in their classroom for Snacks and Games.
- **Closing:** All the early childhood children join together for their very own Closing.

Early Childhood Schedule: Three Rotation Sites

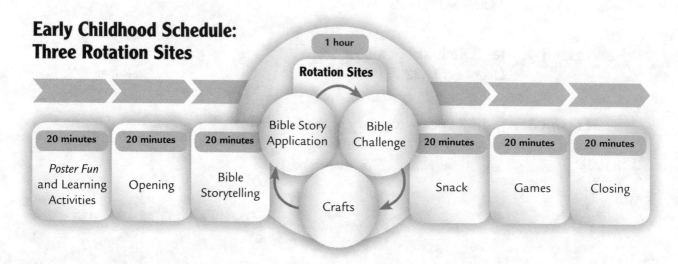

- 20 minutes — *Poster Fun and Learning Activities*
- 20 minutes — Opening
- 20 minutes — Bible Storytelling
- 1 hour — Rotation Sites: Bible Story Application, Bible Challenge, Crafts
- 20 minutes — Snack
- 20 minutes — Games
- 20 minutes — Closing

Option 2: Six Rotation Sites

- All activities are organized into Rotation Sites.
- Children and the grown-ups who brought them do a brief activity together when they arrive. Children then play in thematic Learning Areas.
- All early childhood children gather for the Opening; then they divide into small groups and rotate to six different sites for 20 minutes each:

Bible Storytelling, Bible Story Application, Bible Challenge, Crafts, Snacks, and Games.

- All early childhood children come back together in one large group for Closing.

Early Childhood Schedule: Six Rotation Sites

As children arrive, welcome them with *Poster Fun* and Learning Activities, 20 minutes. Add 5 minutes for travel time between sites.

Site	25 minutes	20 minutes	20 minutes	20 minutes	20 minutes	20 minutes	20 minutes	25 minutes
Opening	All							
Storytelling		Group 1	Group 6	Group 5	Group 4	Group 3	Group 2	
Bible Story Application		Group 2	Group 1	Group 6	Group 5	Group 4	Group 3	
Bible Challenge		Group 3	Group 2	Group 1	Group 6	Group 5	Group 4	
Snacks		Group 4	Group 3	Group 2	Group 1	Group 6	Group 5	
Crafts		Group 5	Group 4	Group 3	Group 2	Group 1	Group 6	
Games		Group 6	Group 5	Group 4	Group 3	Group 2	Group 1	
Closing								All

Barnyard Roundup Course Chart

Bible Stories and Take-Home Points	Bible Memory Verses	Transitions and Activities	Bible Stories 20 minutes	Rotation 1: Bible Story Application 20 minutes
Lesson 1 **Jesus cares, now and forever!** Jesus Is the Good Shepherd *John 10:1–18*	The LORD is my shepherd, I shall not want. *Psalm 23:1*	**Arriving Activities** 20–25 minutes ■ Children & parents do a *Poster Fun* activity as they arrive. ■ Children explore thematic learning areas as others arrive.	Learn that Jesus cares, now and forever!	Use *Lesson 1 Leaflet* to review the story. Use a *Sticker Activity* to explore how Jesus calls us by name and cares for us.
Lesson 2 **Jesus provides, now and forever!** Jesus Feeds 5,000 People *Mark 6:30–44 and John 6:1–14*	He makes me lie down in green pastures. *Psalm 23:2*		Learn that Jesus provides, now and forever!	Use *Lesson 2 Leaflet* to review the story. Use the *Sticker Activity* to learn that Jesus is with us and provides for us.
Lesson 3 **Jesus leads, now and forever!** Jesus Tells about a Sower *Matthew 13:1–23*	He leads me in paths of righteousness. *Psalm 23:3*	**Opening** 20 minutes ■ Meet with all early childhood groups. ■ Hear the Take-Home Point.	Learn that Jesus leads, now and forever!	Use *Lesson 3 Leaflet* to review the story. Use the *Sticker Activity* to learn that Jesus makes our faith grow and leads us.
Lesson 4 **Jesus forgives, now and forever!** Jesus Tells about a Lost Son *Luke 15:11–32*	I will fear no evil, for You are with me. *Psalm 23:4*	■ Sing songs and pray. ■ Greet Polly the Pig; introduce the Bible story theme. ■ Make	Learn that Jesus forgives, now and forever!	Use *Lesson 4 Leaflet* to review the story. Use the *Sticker Activity* to learn how Jesus forgives us, even if we stray.
Lesson 5 **Jesus is our Savior, now and forever!** Jesus Appears to Mary in the Garden *John 20:1–18*	I shall dwell in the house of the LORD forever. *Psalm 23:6*	announcements and give offering.	Learn that Jesus is our Savior, now and forever!	Use *Lesson 5 Leaflet* to review the story. Use the *Sticker Activity* to learn how Jesus is our Savior.

Rotation 2: Bible Challenge 20 minutes	Rotation 3: Crafts 20 minutes	Snacks 20 minutes	Games 20 minutes	Closing 15 minutes
Learn *Psalm 23:1* with a song. Do a shepherd dramatization with song.	**Psalm 23 Frame**	**Follow the Flock**	**Sheep Herding**	
Learn *Psalm 23:2* with a song. Play a sharing game or a circle game.	**Jesus Fish Sand Art**	**Baskets of Blessings**	**Fly the Coop**	All early childhood groups meet.
Learn *Psalm 23:3* with a song. Sing a review song and word-spelling activity.	**Now & Forever Cross**	**Scattering Seeds**	**Count the Corn**	Review Take-Home Point and Bible Story. Sing songs and pray.
Learn *Psalm 23:4* with a song. Play a passing game.	**Forgiven Suncatcher**	**All Mixed Up**	**Feed the Pigs**	Review the Lesson with Polly. Get ready to go home.
Learn *Psalm 23:6* with a song. Use posters to review Bible stories.	**My Savior Kite**	**Let Love Show**	**Gather the Eggs**	Send information home to families.

Site Highlights

A Prayer to Begin

God, our heavenly Father, thank You for working through Your Word to bring me to faith and for keeping me in Your grace. Give me a growing faith, energy, power, wisdom, and patience so I can share the stories about Jesus. Enable me to teach Your Word clearly. During this week, strengthen us with Your Holy Word and work through us to share the Good News about Jesus with these children and their families. In Jesus' name I pray. Amen.

Transition Activities As the Lesson Begins

Welcome

Stand near the door to welcome everyone and ask grown-ups to sign in children. Use the *Sign In & Out Sheet* provided. Give each child a nametag and a sticker to mark attendance, or give each child a sheep with his or her name on it (using the pattern found on the *Leader CD*) and have the child put it in a "pen" (mark off an area on the table) to mark attendance. Help children and parents ease into your area by letting them do the *Poster Fun* activity together before grown-ups leave. Set up a table with supplies and directions for this activity. The poster is the outer wrap of the *Little Sprouts Early Childhood Leaflets* packet.

Activities

Show the children the learning areas you set up ahead of time. Children love the individual, side-by-side, or interactive play of learning areas. Some grown-ups may want to stay and observe for a while. As children become engaged in play, grown-ups usually become more comfortable and able to say good-bye. Grown-ups should inform their children when they leave the room. Sneaking out while children are engaged in play may make the children even more anxious later on.

Activities in learning areas introduce and explore the lesson's Bible story, Take-Home Point, or life application. Each area needs at least one child-size table. Assign Helpers to each area to guide the children and talk with them during the activity. Post simple visuals at the entrance of each learning area. On the sign, you can post a guide for how many children may play there at one time. Site Signs are available on the *Leader CD* in this guide.

The three learning areas are described in each lesson. The first learning area, called Make It, provides activities for the children to use small muscles to explore items that relate to Bible story concepts. Make It activities can be left out from day to day, as space permits. The second learning area, called Imagine It, provides activities so the children can better understand a farming or faith concept. The third learning area, called Act It Out, provides activities so the children can interact with one another and role-play.

Coloring Pages for each day are available on the *Leader CD*. You may wish to use the Coloring Pages as your time begins or later for Bible story review.

Opening (All Early Childhood Groups)

Have one person lead the Opening (the directions are provided in each lesson each day), or rotate responsibilities with other Early Childhood Leaders.

Choose a room that's large enough for all of the early childhood children to gather for Openings and Closings. Set up a small table as an altar, with a battery-operated candle, a cross, and a Bible on it. Make the *Barnyard Roundup* Red Barn Puppet Stage (*Leader CD*) or make a puppet stage from a table covering the top and sides with brown (mud) sheet or craft paper. Secure with tape. Raise the table to a height to hide a seated Puppeteer, or use Polly yourself. A cardboard fence along the top of the table can show Polly's pen. With either stage, the Leader may want to sit on a stool or hay bale while talking to Polly.

Use a bell to call the children to and from Opening each day. As the children enter the room, play music. When everyone is seated, make the candle light to show that it's a special time. Sing suggested songs from the *Leader CD*.

In the Puppet Skits, Polly the Pig introduces the Bible story and theme. Recruit a Puppeteer to operate Polly while a Leader talks to her.

Teach the children to talk to God, or pray, by folding their hands, closing their eyes, and bowing their heads in order to shut out distractions. Ask them to repeat prayer phrases after you. You may choose to say the Apostles' Creed and the Lord's Prayer in the same way. Use actions to help the children remember the words. Have children help collect offerings. Distribute *Barndana Buffs Team Identifiers* to distinguish the groups.

Depending on how you organize your program, you will either take the children to the next Rotation Site or back to their classroom for the Bible story.

Bible Story

Check the daily lists for the items you need each day, including pictures, items, and posters to print from the *Leader CD* in the center of this guide. Hang *Bible Story Posters* around this site.

Rotation Sites

Early Childhood Teams get into the three Rotation Groups. Each Rotation Group moves to their assigned Rotation Site. When it is time to move to a different Rotation Site, whistle or ring the bell three times.

Site 1: Bible Story Application

Children use the *Little Sprouts Early Childhood Leaflets* to do an activity and participate in finger plays, role plays, and other movement activities based on the Bible story. Children can sit on the floor or use a large table with preschool chairs for six or seven children. You might use the same table as the *Poster Fun* activity (when people arrived). Hang up the Bible Story Application Sign from your *Leader CD*.

Add the lesson's Bible Story Coloring Pages from the *Leader CD* here for a visual review and reinforcement of the Bible story.

Site 2: Bible Challenge

The children sing the Bible Memory Verse, using the Bible Memory Songs on the *Leader CD*. Use an open area for these activities, possibly the same one used for Storytelling. Hang up the Bible Challenge Sign from your *Leader CD*.

Site 3: Crafts

Children need a table where they can make craft projects. Set up close to a sink, or have wet wipes and paper towels handy to clean spills and messy fingers. Spread plastic tarps under the tables to protect the floor. Add preschool chairs for six or seven children. Set up another table or area where craft items can dry without disturbance, or hang cords from the ceiling to attach craft projects with clothespins. Hang up the Craft Sign from your *Leader CD*.

Snacks

Ask your VBS Director how to handle snacks. Some programs serve snacks in one area. Others serve the early childhood children in their rooms or outside. If you do snacks in your room, you need a table and chairs here too. See the *Bountiful Blessings Snack Guide* for complete snack suggestions.

Games

Play games in an open area. The games included in the *Bales of Fun Game Guide* reinforce Bible truths. Activities to play as a group and activity centers for a play yard are suggested.

Closing (All Early Childhood Groups)

All early childhood children meet together again for the Closing, usually in the same place they met for Opening. Polly reappears to review what the children learned. Close with a song and prayer, as described in each lesson. Send home the daily leaflet, the *My Shepherd Collectibles*, and each lesson's projects so children can share what they learned with family and friends. Remind the children to be "Son Spotters," using the SONspot activity.

What You Need

Little Sprouts Early Childhood Leaflets
321660

Every child and Early Childhood Leader needs one. Each set contains 5 *Little Sprouts Early Childhood Leaflets,* the *Poster Fun* activities, and stickers for the student activities in this guide.

5 Bible Story Posters, 321696

These large, full-color posters help students focus on the Bible story and provide a visual reminder of God's Word.

Early Childhood Leader Guide with Leader CD, 321600

Every Early Childhood Leader needs one. The *Leader CD* in the guide contains 20 songs. There are 7 songs for your Early Childhood setting, 8 VBS theme songs, and 5 Bible Memory Songs. The *Leader CD* also has print resources, including Bible Story Coloring Pages and Rotation Site Signs.

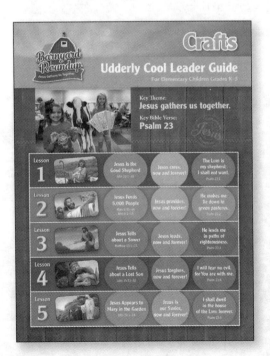

Craft Leader Guide, 321633

This instruction guide will show you how to make Bible story connections with fun, quality crafts (sold separately).

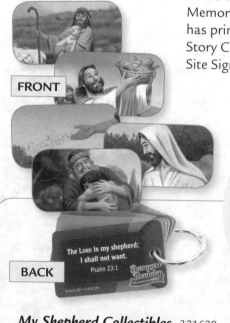

FRONT

BACK

My Shepherd Collectibles, 321620

Send home these great reminders of the Bible Memory Verse each day.

The **House of the Lord Carabiner**, 321617
Holds the collectibles (sold separately).

Polly the Pig Puppet

Polly meets the kids every lesson in the Opening and Closing.

321681

Supply List

In addition to the purchased items on the previous page, these are items you will supply locally or copy from the *Leader CD*.

Every Lesson Supplies

- Bible
- *Leader CD*
- Farm-themed decorations and books
- Carpet squares, 1 for each child, or tablecloths
- Altar with cross, battery-operated candles
- Bell or whistle
- *Barnyard Roundup* Red Barn Puppet Stage (see Opening on p. 8 for description)
- *Polly the Pig Puppet*
- Copies of Puppet Skits for the Puppeteer, Leader, and CD Helper
- CD player
- Crayons, scissors, glue sticks, washable markers
- Wet wipes or access to a sink
- *Sign In & Out Sheet (Leader CD);* one for each session
- Attendance "sheep pen" made by drawing a oval shape on a large piece of paper or putting blocks around the edge (optional, but fun!)
- Sheep shapes, 1 for each child (use the Sheep Pattern from the *Leader CD*, make copies and write each child's name on them) to place in the "sheep pen" to take attendance each lesson (optional)
- Nametags
- Rope with knots (optional)
- Copies of the *Poster Fun* activities for grown-ups to use with kids (*Leader CD*)
- Copies of Lyrics Sheets and *Bible Memory Songs Sign Chart* for Leaders and Helpers (*Leader CD*)
- Copies of Bible Story Coloring Pages (*Leader CD*)
- Snack ingredients for each lesson
- Game items for each lesson
- Craft items for each lesson
- Learning Area supplies (see each lesson's list below and Master Supply List on *Leader CD*)
- Storytelling supplies (see each lesson's list below and Master Supply List on *Leader CD*)

Lesson 1

Learning Area Supplies: 2–5 sheep pens on trays; 2–5 small appetizer tongs; 2–5 bowls of cotton balls; dice (optional); toy animals (farm and wild animals); sheep ears and shepherd staffs (optional); green, blue, and brown towels (optional); sheep pattern (optional)

Storytelling Supplies: Tag labeled "217" for Polly's ear; brown yarn or rope; Shepherd, Thief, and Wolf figures printed from *Leader CD*, attached to craft sticks, and placed in balls of play dough; 1 sheep for each child; green fabric or felt; blue fabric or felt; large stick or cane; bandana

Lesson 2

Learning Area Supplies: plastic tub; green paper; scissors; green Easter grass or green ribbon (optional); 2–3 small blankets; paper plates; many construction-paper cutouts of fish and bread (save for Storytelling supplies); baskets

Storytelling Supplies: 3 small (5-inch) paper plates with Jesus, Disciples, and Boy figures glued on them; wooden craft sticks; construction-paper fish (4) and bread loaves (10); dry beans or rice; tape; 2 beanbags or soft balls (optional)

Lesson 3

Learning Area Supplies: pie tin or small cake pan; various large seeds; muffin pan or egg cartons; 2–4 small tongs; a large blanket

Storytelling Supplies: 4 square cake pans; rocks; mud; weeds; soil; medium-size seeds; a small bag; a dried-up plant; a healthy stalk of grain; pictures of plants (optional); 5 pieces of paper

Lesson 4

Learning Area Supplies: a toy barn; toy farm animals; a plastic tub with green shredded paper (from Lesson 2); a large basket; beanbags; robe (optional)

Storytelling Supplies: white board, marker, bag of coins

Lesson 5

Learning Area Supplies: play dough; small rolling pins; biscuit cutters, round cookie cutters, jar lids, or plastic cups; plastic coffee stirrers or unsharpened pencils; a rhythm instrument

Storytelling Supplies: bandage; small sunflower; 4 paper plates with a face drawn on each; a cross; all 5 *Bible Story Posters*

Advance Preparation for *Barnyard Roundup*

As an Early Childhood Leader, it is your privilege to help young children grow in faith and knowledge of our heavenly Father and Jesus, our Savior, by the power of the Holy Spirit. Here are some things you and your team will want to do before the children arrive for VBS.

To-Do Check List

▨ Pray for your children and their families, your early childhood team, and yourself.

▨ Review the resources you'll need in this guide and on the *Leader CD* in this guide. These tools will make your planning and teaching easy and fun!

▨ Prepare nametags for children and Helpers.

▨ Read the Scripture and Leader Devotion to prepare for each lesson.

▨ Read through all the lessons.

▨ Coordinate activities and responsibilities with other Early Childhood Leaders, especially Openings and Closings.

▨ Delegate tasks. Ask Helpers to work in a learning area or Rotation Site, be Puppeteers for Openings and Closings, or care for a special group of children.

▨ Have a volunteer cut apart the stickers from the *Little Sprouts Early Childhood Leaflets* and put them in plastic zipper bags labeled with the day and the activity.

▨ Plan your Puppet Skits. Ask a Helper to work the *Polly the Pig Puppet*. (You could do it by yourself if necessary.) Copy Puppet Scripts for your Helper.

▨ Copy other pages you need from the Leader Guide (e.g., *Poster Fun* activities and Rotation-Site directions) and print CD resources, such as forms and posters, from the *Leader CD*.

▨ Gather materials and make props.

▨ Decorate your area with farm-theme items.

▨ Check supply lists to see what you need.

Gather a Great Idea!

Use high school students or older volunteers to supervise learning areas. This frees you up to greet parents and students.

▨ Practice presentations, including puppet skits.

▨ Prepare the resources you need for introducing and telling the stories.

▨ To move the early childhood children to various sites, make ropes. Take a length of rope, about 2 foot per child, and add knots about every eighteen inches. Jump ropes or rope from home-improvement stores work well. The Leader holds one end of the rope and leads. The children hold on to the rope at the knot and walk from one place to another.

▨ Gather the local supplies.

▨ Set up and decorate the early childhood space.

▨ Use your church's child protection procedures. If your church hasn't defined procedures, ask your VBS Director for guidance.

▨ Copy the *Sign In & Out Sheet* to use every day (*Leader CD*). Ask parents to list people who have permission to take the children and provide phone numbers and contact information. Ask anyone you do not personally know to show a photo ID. Do not allow older siblings to bring or pick up children.

▨ Attend VBS staff training.

Share the Take-Home Point!

VBS Leaders lead the children in the lesson's Take-Home Point Call and Response. Here's what to say and do! You, the Leader, point up and circle your hand twice and say, **GATHER 'ROUND!** Then point up and say the lesson's Take-Home Point, **JESUS CARES!** The Teams join you, and all of you point up and repeat, **JESUS CARES!** Everyone then makes a circle with their hand as they say, **NOW AND FOREVER!** Practice this! (The "Jesus" part changes for each lesson, but the actions remain the same!)

LEADER: GATHER 'ROUND! (Point up and circle hand.) **JESUS CARES! KIDS AND LEADERS:** (Point up.) **JESUS CARES,** (Circle hand.) **NOW AND FOREVER!**

Make VBS Work for You and Your Kids!

Consider your unique situation. Look at the following suggestions to help you adjust the program to fit your needs, based on factors such as group size and location:

Use Transition Activities in Different Ways

- Use Transition Activities *more often*, for a longer period of time at the beginning of the day and/or include time for the Transition Activities at the end of the day. You may want to extend the time given to children to do the Make It activity.

- Provide *more* free play activities/learning areas (that are not teacher-directed). Provide other things children can play with during Transition Activities, such as blocks, Duplo pieces, play dough, or other tabletop manipulatives. Each day, include an activity like a sensory table as a choice during the free-play time. It can have the same materials in it each day, or it can be a different sensory experience each day.

- Consider how lengthening or adding to the Transition Activities affects Opening and Closing and your drop-off and pick-up procedure.

Use Rotation Sites in Different Ways

- Instead of moving to a different site/location in your facility for Crafts and Snacks, have Helpers bring the supplies to your room and set up the activity for you at a table at a predetermined time. Supplies could be transported with a cart. Supplies could even be individually prepackaged in gallon-size plastic zipper bags for each child.

- Use the sites as st[...] play time. Allow the [...] their own schedule. [...] with smaller groups o[...] stations at once. Do th[...] as a whole group, but B[...] (leaflets), Bible Challeng[...] ...ks can be used as teacher-led tab[...] ...s (centers). Close with the Games and Closing as a whole group.

- Expand your active Games time by doing the suggested game and the *Fun in the Play Yard* activity. Or add free-play time on the playground that isn't teacher-directed.

- If trying to adapt the Leader Guide for even younger children (e.g., the children of volunteers, in a nursery), choose only a few of the activities/sites (e.g., Snack and the music from Bible Challenge). Do not try to use all of the ideas.

Think about Young Children's Needs

- Young children may not be able to listen well at Opening or Storytelling. Have several finger plays (action poems) ready to use to recapture their attention and give them time to move. Think of ways to involve those children as your "helpers" (e.g., hold up a prop, point to something). Use your volunteer Helpers strategically; tell them which children need to sit on a Helper's lap during listening times. Have sensory objects (e.g., a soft, stuffed sheep toy) ready for them to hold, so they have something to finger while they're listening.

- Young children may need help with the lesson leaflet activity. Pair younger three-year-olds with older five-year-olds. Only pass out the daily stickers (cut apart from each lesson's stickers), not the whole sheet to manipulate. Consider letting the children lie on their stomachs on the floor to do the activity instead of exclusively working at tables.

- If you do not have a restroom in your room, provide for several opportunities during the day for children to use the restroom besides the one time indicated at the Snack rotation.

- Balance loud, active times with quieter times. For example, after Games, children may listen well for the Closing. Use storytelling and quiet music to create a calmer atmosphere.

Lesson 1

Roundup Leader Devotion

Bible Story: Jesus Is the Good Shepherd
John 10:1–18

Bible Memory Verse:
"The LORD is my shepherd; I shall not want." Psalm 23:1

Read John 10:1–18 and
Think on These Things:

The parable of the Good Shepherd stands near the center of the Gospel of John.

John 10:1–6 Jesus begins this parable with a job description of a shepherd. A shepherd enters the sheepfold by the door. His sheep recognize his voice, and he knows their names. A thief or robber climbs in for evil purposes! A stranger calls, but the sheep won't follow. Instead, they head the other way!

John 10:7–10 Then Jesus says, "I am the door of the sheep" (v. 7). He distinguishes Himself from those who came before Him. He is the door through which we enter to find green pasture and abundant life.

John 10:11–18 Having described the job of a shepherd, Jesus takes it up a notch and declares, "I am the good shepherd"—not just once, but twice. A good shepherd lays down his life for the sheep. A good shepherd knows his sheep, and they know him. Our Good Shepherd does the will of His Father. He lays down His life and gathers the sheep into one flock with one Shepherd. That's the Good Shepherd's job description, as given by God the Father.

Jesus is our Good Shepherd. Even when we wander away in sin—and especially because we are vulnerable to attacks by sin and Satan—Jesus cares for us, protects us, provides for us, and is with us all the times. What's our response? We give Him thanks and praise for His gracious and abundant care.

Take-Home Point:
Jesus cares, now and forever!

When kids get scared, they need someone to care for them. They need someone who comes alongside them to help. They need someone to protect them and provide what they need. God gives us people in this life to do that: parents and family, pastors and teachers, friends and neighbors. Jesus cares. He is with us. He provides for us. He protects. His care is for today and for all eternity. We need Jesus.

Jesus Gathers Us Together: As the Good Shepherd, Jesus gathers us together in His Church. He takes care of all our needs, now and forever. He takes care of us by protecting us from sin and Satan. He takes care of

us by providing for all our needs of body and soul. He laid down His life for us, giving us forgiveness of sins, eternal life, and salvation through the Word and in the Sacraments.

Prayer: Jesus, You are the Good Shepherd. You care for us, and You care for the kids who are coming to VBS. We were as helpless as sheep against the enemies of sin, Satan, and death, but You provided protection and salvation, now and forever. Lead us to follow You just as sheep follow their shepherd. Bless our time with these kids as they learn about You and Your care. In Your holy name we pray. Amen.

Jesus Is the Good Shepherd

John 10:1–18

Lesson 1

Take-Home Point

Jesus cares, now and forever!

Today You Need

Leader and Student Materials (p. 10)

Every Lesson Supplies (p. 11)

Learning Area Supplies: 2–5 sheep pens on trays; 2–5 small appetizer tongs; 2–5 bowls of cotton balls; dice (optional); toy animals (farm and wild animals); sheep ears and shepherd staffs (optional); green, blue, and brown towels (optional); sheep pattern (optional)

Storytelling Supplies: Tag labeled "217" for Polly's ear; brown yarn or rope; Shepherd, Thief, and Wolf figures printed from *Leader CD*, attached to craft sticks, and placed in balls of play dough; 1 sheep for each child; green fabric or felt; blue fabric or felt; large stick or cane; bandana

See the Master Supply List on *Leader CD* for complete list for all lessons.

Welcome, *Poster Fun*, and Learning Areas

🕐 **20 minutes**

Play music from the *Leader CD* in the background. Have Helpers with nametags stationed inside and outside of the entrance to greet and direct families to the welcome table. While helping children with nametags and attendance stickers, ask the parents/caregivers to use the *Sign In & Out Sheet* each day. Have the children put their sheep in the sheep pen to take attendance.

SAY: Hi, I'm (Leader's name). (Child's name), **welcome to *Barnyard Roundup*! We'll do so many fun activities here. We'll learn about Jesus and His love for us. We'll hear how He is with us, providing for us and protecting us. You can go to the *Poster Fun* table. The Helpers will give you the posters and directions.**

Poster Fun Helpers give out posters and directions. Make sure first and last names are printed on the posters. Remind parents to leave the posters on the table before moving to the next activity. Helpers will gather and sort posters alphabetically by last name to prepare for Lesson 2.

Arranging the classroom: You may choose to decorate the classroom as a barnyard. In addition to the learning areas, you may set up an area for pretend play that includes farm toys and blocks for creating pens and barns. Another quiet area can have several farm-themed books in a basket. Be sure to include children's Bibles and Bible story books that reflect the lessons for the week. Carpet squares or tablecloths work well to define seating areas. You will need a bell to use for transition times. A cowbell would fit the farm theme, but singing, playing a few notes on a recorder or flute, or using a "sheepdog" puppet would be a more accurate representation of rounding up sheep.

Poster Fun for Parents and Kids

You need: *Poster Fun*, pencil or pen, brown crayons, and *Shepherd Sticker*

Parents: Print your child's first and last name on the front. Look at the picture on the front with your child. **SAY: Look at this farm picture! At *Barnyard Roundup*, you will learn all kinds of things about being on a farm. What do you see in the picture?** Allow your child to point out things that are familiar to him or her.

Turn over the poster to the back page. Have your child repeat the Lesson 1 Bible Memory Verse after you. Point to the Lesson 1 shepherd's staff icon. **SAY: Shepherds use this special tool, called a staff, to protect sheep from other animals that might hurt them. God's Word helps us learn about Jesus, our Good Shepherd, who protects us. Color the staff brown.**

Open *Poster Fun* and point to the Lesson 1 picture. **SAY: What animal do you see? If you touch a sheep, how does it feel?**

Show the *Shepherd Sticker*. **SAY: A person who takes care of sheep is called a shepherd. Put the *Shepherd Sticker* near the sheep to take care of it. In your story today, you will learn about a special shepherd—the Good Shepherd. It is Jesus! You will learn how the shepherd cares for the sheep and how Jesus cares for us. Repeat after me: JESUS CARES, NOW AND FOREVER.**

Leave the activity on the table. Take your child to Learning Area 1. Once your child is engaged in the activity, you may quietly leave.

Transition Activities

Learning Area 1: Make It
Put the Sheep in the Pen

Goal: Use fine motor muscles to put cotton-ball sheep in a pen. The Good Shepherd guards the sheepfold and cares for the sheep.

You need: 2–5 sheep pens (ovals drawn along the edges of a piece of paper; make as simple or detailed as desired) on trays; 2–5 small plastic or wooden appetizer tongs; 2–5 bowls of cotton balls; dice (optional)

SAY: Jesus tells us that He is the Good Shepherd who cares for us. A shepherd takes care of the sheep in the sheep pen and makes sure they stay safe. We will pretend to put sheep in a sheep pen. Share the Take-Home Point and **SAY: GATHER 'ROUND!** (Point up and circle hand.) **JESUS CARES! TEAMS:** (Point up.) **JESUS CARES,** (Circle hand.) **NOW AND FOREVER!**

Set out a tray holding a sheep pen, a set of tongs, and a bowl of cotton balls. You may need two to five trays, depending on the size of your group. Children use the tongs to pick up cotton balls and move them inside the pen. Model the activity, as needed. Older preschoolers may enjoy rolling a die, counting the dots and then putting that number of "sheep" in the pen.

Learning Area Options:

Have blank pieces of paper and crayons available. Helpers can encourage children to draw a sheep pen and glue cotton balls inside the pen. They can draw a "good shepherd" (stick person) outside the pen by drawing a person holding a shepherd's staff. **SAY: The good shepherd uses this special tool, called a staff, to help guide the sheep where they need to go or to rescue them if they are in danger.**

Bible Story Coloring Pages (*Leader CD*): Use the lesson's Coloring Page. Helpers can encourage the children to identify the objects and person on the Coloring Page. Then they can tell the children that they will be hearing this Bible story a little later.

Learning Area 2: Imagine It
Animal Sort

Goal: The children will learn about animals that live on farms by separating them from wild animals.

You need: toy animals, both farm and wild animals (optional: provide photos of animals printed from the Internet)

SAY: God made many wonderful animals. Look at these animals. Can you tell me the names of some of the animals that God made? Have them say the names of animals they know. **SAY: Are any of these animals alike?** Compare. Allow the children to sort the animals any way they like. **SAY: Which of these animals might live on a farm? Can you make the sounds of farm animals? What are some things farm animals need?** (Discuss. Guide the children to know that animals need food, water, and shelter.) **Do we need those things too?** (Yes) **Who takes care of animals on a farm?** (A farmer) **Do you know what the special word is for a person who takes care of sheep?** (Shepherd)

SAY: In our Bible story today, we are going to hear about a shepherd taking care of His sheep. Jesus said that He is the Good Shepherd, who takes care of us!

Learning Area 3: Act It Out
Caring for Sheep

Goal: The children act out caring for sheep like a shepherd as they get to know one another's names.

You need: nothing (optional: sheep ears for the sheep, some shepherd staffs or walking sticks for the shepherds, a green towel for grass, a blue towel for water, and a brown towel for a sheep pen)

Divide the children into two equal groups. One group will be sheep; the other will be shepherds. Assign one sheep to one shepherd. Assure the children that after a while, they will be able to trade roles. If your group is small, you could be the shepherd and the children the sheep; let each child take a turn being the shepherd.

SAY: Sheep, I need you to get down on your hands and knees. What sound does a sheep make? Continue, **Shepherds, it is your job to take care of the sheep. It is very important that you know your sheep's name so you can call your sheep to come to you.** Help the children learn one another's names. **SAY: What do sheep eat?** If children can't guess, **SAY: It is green and it grows in your front yard.** Once they guess grass, **SAY: Sheep can't find grass by themselves. So shepherds, lead your sheep to some grass.** Pretend a spot in your room is grass; shepherds lead the sheep there. **SAY: What else do sheep need?** Help the shepherds guide their sheep to some "water" and a "sheep pen." **SAY: You were such good shepherds. You took good care of your sheep! You made sure they had what they needed and that they were safe. Jesus is our Good Shepherd. He makes sure we have what we need and that we are safe, now and forever.**

Opening

🕐 20 minutes

You need: a small table for an altar area (this could be as simple as a plastic crate turned over with a cloth on top, a cross and a battery-operated candle to place on the altar), Lyrics Sheets, *Leader CD*, Puppet Scripts and props, *Polly the Pig Puppet*, bell, Bible

Ring the bell to get everyone's attention. **SING** (to the tune of "*The Farmer in the Dell*"):

> It's Bible story time. It's Bible story time.
> We're going to hear how Jesus cares.
> It's Bible story time!

Repeat as needed, encouraging the children to sing along as they move toward the altar area and are seated.

SAY: I am so happy to have you joining us for our *Barnyard Roundup*! We have already had some fun, and we will be having more fun later. But now we have the most important part of our day. It is when we get to hear what God tells us in His book, the **Bible.** Hold up the Bible.

Show the children how to fold their hands. **SAY: In the name of the Father and of the Son and of the Holy Spirit. Amen. We say those words to remember that God is with us. Now I am going to light the candle to remind us that Jesus is the Light. The sun shines every day, and Jesus shines on us every day!** Light the candle.

SING: "I Am Jesus' Little Lamb" (*Leader CD* Track 15). Add the following actions:

I am Jesus' little lamb, (*Put hand out in front of body, palm down. Bounce your hand from right to left.*)

Ever glad at heart I am; (*Touch heart and smile.*)

For my Shepherd gently guides me, (*Put hand in front of body, palm toward tummy. Take other hand and grab tips of fingers. Use that hand to gently pull palm from right to left.*)

Knows my need (*Point to head with index finger.*)

and well provides me, (*Sweep hand across front of body.*)

Loves me ev'ry day the same, (*Hug self.*)

Even calls me by my name. (*Keep arms around self or touch heart. Nod on each beat. On "name," stick out index finger and middle finger of each hand, keeping the two together; place one hand on top of the other hand; tap twice.*)

Teach the Take-Home Point

SAY: Who cares for you? How do you know they care for you? Give the children time to discuss. **SAY: Because we know Jesus cares for us, we don't need to worry or be afraid. Jesus takes care of everything we need. He even takes care of our biggest need— protecting us from our enemies sin and the devil. Each day, we have peace because we know Jesus is with us and is caring for us, all the time.**

SAY: Here at *Barnyard Roundup*, we have a special way of reminding one another of how God has gathered us together to be His children. Let's stand up. When you hear me or one of the Helpers say, "GATHER 'ROUND! JESUS CARES!" while pointing up and making a circle with our hand like this (demonstrate), **then you will all say, "JESUS CARES, NOW AND FOREVER!"** while doing the same motion. Let's try it. **Are you ready?**

SAY: GATHER 'ROUND! (Point up and circle hand.) **JESUS CARES! KIDS AND LEADERS:** (Point up.) **JESUS CARES,** (Circle hand.) **NOW AND FOREVER!** Now let's do it again in a whisper voice. Repeat Take-Home Point. **Now let's do it in our loudest voice.** Repeat Take-Home Point.

Pray

Have the children sit down. **SAY: Now let's talk to God by praying.** Invite the children to fold their hands, bow their heads, and repeat each phrase of the prayer after you. Pause after each forward slash mark (/).

SAY: Jesus, / You are our Good Shepherd. / Help us to listen / and learn / how much You care for us. / We trust in You, Jesus. / Amen.

Opening Puppet Skit

You need: stage, shelf, or table for the puppet skit; *Polly the Pig Puppet*, Puppet Script (*Leader CD*), puppet prop

Summary: Pig 217 becomes Polly the Pig when she comes to a new farm, and she starts to understand how much the farmer there cares for her.

After the skit, **SAY: I am so glad Polly got a name, aren't you? And I'm glad she has come to a farm where she will be taken care of. Now let's hear what Jesus had to say about how the Good Shepherd cares for His sheep. Now it's time for our Storytelling.**

Bible Storytelling

🕐 **20 minutes**

You need: Bible; a piece of brown yarn or rope that will form the sheep pen; Shepherd, Thief, and Wolf figures (*Leader CD*) from the *Lesson 1 Bible Story Poster* and glued or taped onto a wooden craft stick and placed in a ball of play dough so they can stand up; 1 sheep for each child (e.g., plastic sheep, sheep figures printed from the *Leader CD*, pictures of sheep, cotton balls); a piece of green felt or fabric for the green pasture; a round or oval piece of blue fabric or felt for the still water

Note: *Lesson 1 Bible Story Poster* is also available as clip art on your *Leader CD*.

Seat the children in a circle so you can tell the story by placing the props on the floor in front of you. Give each child a sheep. Cue your Helper to assist as needed, moving props or saying the sheep names.

Hold up the Bible and **SAY: In the Bible, Jesus tells us that He is the Good Shepherd who cares for His sheep. Do you know who His sheep are? You! I am going to give you each a sheep to help me tell the story.**

Use a piece of yarn or rope to make a circle on the floor. **SAY: This is a sheep pen. It is also called a sheepfold. It is a wall or a fence. Why do you think the sheep need to be in a pen?** (So they won't get lost and so wild animals can't get to them) **I would like each of you to put your sheep in the sheepfold. Say the name of your sheep as you put it in. Your sheep should have your name.**

As children put the sheep in the pen, **SING** (to the tune of "The Farmer in the Dell," singing "(The)" on the upbeat):

> **The sheep are in the pen.**
> **The sheep are in the pen.**
> **(The) Shepherd will care for them.**
> **The sheep are in the pen.**

Bring out the Shepherd figure. **SAY: Here is a good shepherd. I wonder why we call him a good shepherd instead of a bad shepherd?** (He takes care of his sheep; if he was a bad shepherd, he would not.) **How does the good shepherd take good care of the sheep? What is something that sheep need?** (Food) **What do sheep like to eat?** (Grass) **Do you think there is grass to eat inside the sheep pen?** (No, the shepherd has to take the sheep out of the pen to find grass.) **A place with nice green grass for animals to eat is called a pasture.** Move the shepherd to lead the sheep out of the pen to the grass. Have the shepherd call the name of each sheep. **Jesus said that the good shepherd calls his sheep by name and they follow him.**

As you are moving the sheep, **SING** (to the tune of "The Farmer in the Dell"):

> **The sheep will go and eat.**
> **The sheep will go and eat.**
> **(The) Shepherd leads them out to eat.**
> **The sheep will go and eat.**

SAY: What do sheep need if they are thirsty? (Water) **Where will they get water?** Suggest silly possibilities. (No, the shepherd will have to lead them to a river or stream to drink.) Have the Shepherd call the names of the sheep and lead them from the pasture to the water.

As the sheep are moving, **SING** (to the tune of "The Farmer in the Dell"):

> **The sheep will go and drink.**
> **The sheep will go and drink.**
> **(The) Shepherd leads them out to drink.**
> **The sheep will go and drink.**

Have the Wolf figure approach the sheep. **SAY: Oh no, here comes a wolf! What do you think the wolf wants to do?** (Eat the sheep.) **The sheep are all running away to get away from the wolf.** Scatter the sheep yourself. **What will the good shepherd do? Will he run away?** (No) Have the good shepherd chase the wolf away. Then have the shepherd call the sheep back by name. **Jesus says the good shepherd will not let the wolf get the sheep. He would even die before he would let the wolf get to the sheep, he loves them so.** Lay the shepherd across the gate.

As you are moving the sheep, **SING** (to the tune of "The Farmer in the Dell"):

> **The Shepherd keeps them safe.**
> **The Shepherd keeps them safe.**
> **He'd give His life for them.**
> **The Shepherd keeps them safe.**

Show the Thief figure, sneaking up to the sheep pen from the side. **SAY: Who is this?** Make the figure jump over the fence and approach the sheep. **This man is going to try to steal some sheep! He is called a thief. A thief takes things from others that don't belong to him. Will the sheep follow him?** (The sheep don't know the thief, so they won't follow him.) Have the good shepherd chase the thief away. **SAY: How do you think the sheep feel, knowing their good shepherd protected them from the thief?** (Thankful and happy! They love him and want to only follow him.) **SAY: Aren't you glad that Jesus is *your* Good Shepherd?**

Ring the bell and **SAY: It's time to move. Follow your Leaders.**

Rotation Sites

 1 hour

Early Childhood Teams get into three Rotation Groups. Each Rotation Group moves to their assigned Rotation Site. When it is time to move to a different Rotation Site, ring a bell three times.

Rotation 1: Bible Story Application

🕐 **About 20 minutes**

Review

You need: *Lesson 1 Little Sprouts Early Childhood Leaflet* and stickers, crayons

Give *Lesson 1 Little Sprouts Early Childhood Leaflets* to small-group Leaders. Sit at tables or on carpet squares in a circle on the floor. Make sure each child's name gets on his or her leaflet. As you pass out each one, **SAY: This is for Jesus' little lamb** (name of child). When all the leaflets are distributed, **SAY: Can you point to your name? Who knows your name? Jesus, the Good Shepherd knows your name! You are one of His precious sheep.**

SAY: Look at the picture. Do you think this is the city or the country? (The country) **Do sheep live in the city or the country?** (The country) **I spy with my little eye something green that sheep like to eat. Can you point to it?** (Yes, grass.) **I spy with my little eye something blue that sheep like to drink. Can you point to it?** (Yes, water.) **I spy with my little eye someone who cares for sheep. What is he called?** (Yes, the good shepherd.) **Let's look inside the leaflet.**

Leaflet Activity

Pass out the stickers for Lesson 1.

SAY: Point to the drawing of the sheep. Who is with the sheep? (Yes, the good shepherd.) **The good shepherd cares for the sheep. What is one way he cares for the sheep?** He feeds them. **Do you see a sticker with food that sheep like to eat?** (Children point to the *Grass Sticker*). **Yes, put the *Grass Sticker* on the top circle by the sheep, outlined in red.**

What is another way the shepherd cares for the sheep? (He takes them to the water.) **Do you see a sticker with the kind of water sheep like to drink?** (Children point to the *Pond Sticker*). **Let's put the *Pond Sticker* on the blue circle under the *Grass Sticker*.**

What if a bad wolf tries to chase the sheep or eat them? (The shepherd will protect the sheep.) **Do you see the *Wolf Sticker*?** (Children point to it).

I wonder why that red stripe is across the wolf? (It means no more wolf!) **The shepherd will chase him away and bring the sheep back together. Put the *Wolf Sticker* on the green bottom circle by the sheep.**

Now look at the other side of the page. Do you see the boy and girl? (Yes) **Does the Good Shepherd care for boys and girls?** (Yes) **Who is the Good Shepherd?** (Jesus!) **Jesus cares for us, now and forever.**

Look at the rest of the stickers. Which sticker shows that Jesus, our Good Shepherd, gives us food to eat? (Children point to the *Plate of Food Sticker*). **Put the food sticker on the top red circle next to the boy and girl. Which sticker shows that Jesus provides water for us?** (Children point to the *Glass of Water Sticker*). **Put that sticker on the middle blue circle. What is the last sticker?** (A cross) **Remember how Jesus said the good shepherd would die for the sheep? Jesus died on the cross for us to take our sins away. Then He came alive again so we can live with Him forever. So we know that our Good Shepherd cares for us, now and forever! Put the *Cross Sticker* on the bottom circle.**

Now use your crayons to finish coloring the scene. As the children work, compare the sheep's food and water to the boy and girl's food and water. Compare the wolf to our enemies. **The good shepherd chases away wolves that would hurt his sheep. Our Good Shepherd, Jesus, protects us from death by giving His life for us. Let's say our *Take-Home Point* again:**

SAY: GATHER 'ROUND! (Point up and circle hand.) **JESUS CARES! KIDS AND LEADERS:** (Point up.) **JESUS CARES,** (Circle hand.) **NOW AND FOREVER!**

SING (to the tune of "Bingo"):

> **I have a God who knows my name**
> **And Jesus is His name. Yay!** (*Pump fist into the air.*)
> **J-E-S-U-S, J-E-S-U-S, J-E-S-U-S,**
> **And Jesus is His name. Yay!** (*Pump fist into the air.*)

Or **SING:** "We Plow the Fields and Scatter" (*Leader CD* Track 19) as a thank-You song.

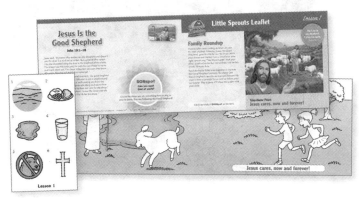

Rotation 2: Bible Challenge

🕐 **About 20 minutes**

The Bible Memory Song

You need: Bible with the Bible Memory Verse marked, *Bible Memory Songs Sign Chart*, *Leader CD*, and CD player

SAY: Our Bible Memory Verse is "The LORD is my shepherd, I shall not want," Psalm 23:1. Those words are from God's book, the Bible. Let's sing this Bible Memory Verse together. Play *Leader CD* Track 9. Add the motions as shown on the *Bible Memory Songs Sign Chart*, from the *Leader CD*.

Story Review

You need: large stick or cane to be a shepherd's staff; bandana to put on the thief's head

Choose one child to be a Wolf, one to be a Thief, and one to be a Good Shepherd. The rest will be Sheep. The first time through, if you have Helpers, they can take the parts of the Shepherd, Wolf, and Thief so the children see what to do.

To the Wolf, **SAY: When it's your turn, can you show me your meanest scariest wolf face and growl?** To the Thief, **SAY: When it's your turn, try to get the Sheep to follow you instead of the Shepherd.** The Shepherd will stand with his or her staff. While helping the Sheep to line up behind the Shepherd, **SING** (to the tune of "Ten Little Indians," with the same syllable emphasis):

> **One little, two little, three little soft sheep.**
> **Four little, five little, six little soft sheep.**
> **Seven little, eight little, nine little soft sheep.**
> **All sheep will follow Me.** ("*Round up*" *all the Sheep behind you.*)

The Sheep follow the Shepherd while singing.

> **Our Shepherd leads all the sheep to the green grass.**
> **Our Shepherd leads all the sheep to the water.**
> **Our Shepherd gives all the sheep all that's needed.**
> **All sheep will follow Me.**

The Wolf comes toward the Sheep and they scatter.

> **Wolves may come lurking around to attack sheep.**
> **Wolves may come lurking around to attack sheep.**
> **Wolves may come lurking around to attack sheep.**
> **So they all run away.**

The Shepherd scares the Wolf away, gathers the Sheep, and leads them back to the beginning.

> **Our Shepherd will give His life to protect them.**
> **Our Shepherd will give His life to protect them.**
> **Our Shepherd will give His life to protect them.**
> **For He loves them so dear.**

Now the Thief comes to beckon some of the Sheep to follow him. The Sheep go to the Shepherd instead.

> **Thieves try to sneak in the pen and snatch sheep up.**
> **Thieves try to sneak in the pen and snatch sheep up.**
> **Thieves try to sneak in the pen and snatch sheep up.**
> **They'll stay with the Shepherd.**

> **Jesus said that He is our good, kind Shepherd.**
> **Jesus said that He is our good, kind Shepherd.**
> **Jesus said that He is our good, kind Shepherd.**
> **We trust and love Him so!**

As time allows, allow other children to play the lead parts.

SAY: GATHER 'ROUND! (Point up and circle hand.) **JESUS CARES! KIDS AND LEADERS:** (Point up) **JESUS CARES,** (Circle hand.) **NOW AND FOREVER! Now let's do it again in a whisper voice.** (Repeat Take-Home Point.) **Now let's do it in our loudest voice.** (Repeat Take-Home Point.)

Rotation 3: Crafts

🕐 **About 20 minutes**

Psalm 23 Frame

You Need

- ▨ *Psalm 23 Frame*, 1 per person
- ▨ Fine-point permanent markers
- ▨ Glue
- ▨ Photo or colored picture (optional)
- ▨ Smocks (optional)
- ▨ Newspaper or disposable plastic tablecloth
- ▨ Tape
- ▨ Finished sample craft

Make It!

Gather needed materials. Write each child's name on the back of his or her frame. Cover the workspace surface with newspaper or a plastic tablecloth and tape down. Show children the supplies and markers. Help and encourage the children as needed.

Children use markers to color the frame. Closely supervise the children's use of the permanent markers. If desired, have the children wear smocks (or large shirts) to protect clothing.

Help children remove the Psalm 23 die-cut shapes from the frame.

Help children glue the shapes to the frame.

Help children glue a photo or a picture they have colored to the middle of the frame.

Putting It All Together

Welcome kids as they arrive. Introduce yourself and any volunteers working in your area.

SAY: GATHER 'ROUND! (Point up and circle hand.)
JESUS CARES! KIDS AND LEADERS: (Point up.)
JESUS CARES, (Circle hand.) **NOW AND FOREVER!**

SAY: Jesus is our Good Shepherd. He calls us by name in Baptism, and through His Word He invites us to follow Him. He takes care of us and provides for all our needs, now and forever.

As you work on your *Psalm 23 Frame*, think about the words of Psalm 23 and what they mean for your life. How has Jesus taken care of you this past week? Did you have food to eat? a place to sleep? Thank Him for these blessings. What worries or troubles do you have? Is a friend being mean to you? Are you worried about something you did that was wrong? Is someone you love sick?

Remember, you are not alone. Jesus, your Good Shepherd, cares for you, now and forever! He gives you what you need to live. He forgives your sins and protects you from your enemies: sin, death, and the devil.

You can talk to Him about everything and trust Him to answer in a way that is best. You can listen to His voice as He talks to you in His Word. Through God's Word, He gives you strength and peace. Through God's Word, you'll know He loves you. It's a love so big that He laid down His life for you so you could have life everlasting with Him. You'll live with Him forever!

Share the "Make It!" instructions and any additional instructions with the students. Point out the supplies on each table, and let the kids create. Craft Leaders and Early Childhood Leaders help and encourage individuals as needed.

Note: The die-cut shapes have numerals by them indicating the order of the text. Do not expect young children to put the text of Psalm 23 in order. Also, note that not all of the text of Psalm 23 is included on the shapes, but all five Bible Memory Verses are referenced.

Snack

🕐 20 minutes

Follow the Flock

You Need

- A plate for each child
- A wooden craft stick and toothpick for each child
- 7 small cauliflower florets for each child
- 2 black olives for each child
- Assorted vegetables to serve on the side, such as carrot sticks, cucumber slices, cherry tomatoes, and bell pepper slices
- Ranch dressing or veggie dip
- A small cup with dip for each child
- A finished example
- Hand sanitizer & napkins
- Cups & water

Advance Preparation

Clean and dry the vegetables. Cut cauliflower into small florets. Each child needs seven florets. For each child, cut one black olive into one small piece for an ear and four long pieces for legs. Cut and prepare other vegetables, such as carrot sticks and cucumber slices, if desired. Before the session, put items listed above on the table(s).

When Kids Arrive

Take the children to the restroom. Have them wash their hands. Have them sit in their places.

SAY: Let's make a snack to help us remember Jesus cares. Let's say the Bible verse: "The LORD is my shepherd; I shall not want." Psalm 23:1. Sheep follow their shepherd. Did you know sheep stick together? They like to stay in a large group—a flock—and follow one another. Sticking together helps protect sheep from their enemies. Sheep want to follow a friendly person who will protect them and lead them to food and water. Jesus, our Good Shepherd, takes care of us and protects us from sin and the devil. Jesus cares, now and forever!

Making the Snack

SAY: To help you remember that Jesus cares for you, we're making a snack that looks like a sheep. Show a finished example. Point to each section of the sheep as you explain:

- Use the white cauliflower to make the sheep's body. Put the pieces in an oval shape in the middle of your plate.
- Place a big black olive on one side to be the sheep's face. Set a small piece of black olive on the head to be an ear.
- Place the four long pieces of black olive on the bottom of the sheep for its legs.
- Dip a toothpick into the dressing and draw an eye on your sheep's face.
- Make a pasture by putting green vegetables around the plate. Make flowers by adding tomatoes or red peppers.

After explaining the snack to the children, demonstrate step-by-step again. Work together as a class, one step at a time, until each child has completed the same step, and then go on at the same time.

SAY: Now dip your veggies in the dressing and enjoy. Jesus, our Good Shepherd, cares for us by providing this healthy food. Say a snack prayer and eat.

Before They Go

SAY: GATHER 'ROUND! (Point up and circle hand.) **JESUS CARES! KIDS AND LEADERS:** (Point up.) **JESUS CARES,** (Circle hand.) **NOW AND FOREVER!**
SAY: Today, you learned how sheep like to stay together. And you learned more about Jesus, our Good Shepherd, who gathers us together and takes care of us.

Games

🕐 **20 minutes**

Sheep Herding

You Need

▨ 6 white balloons and lots of extras (They'll pop!) (optional: permanent marker, curly ribbon, tape)

▨ 4 long-handled flyswatters

▨ 8 hay bales or cones

Get Ready

To prepare for this relay, blow up white balloons to be the sheep. Give them faces and wool marks with permanent markers, or tape on curly ribbon for tails. Have extra balloons ready for those that pop. Set up two cones or hay bales for each line, one at the start, and one about ten feet away, in front of the line.

Here We Go

SAY: **Welcome to Bales of Fun Games! We are glad to have you here with us, learning how Jesus gathers us together. In today's Bible story, we are talking about Jesus, our Good Shepherd. How do shepherds take care of their sheep?** (They lead their sheep to food and water and protect them from danger.) **Shepherds care for their sheep, and Jesus cares for us!**

SAY: GATHER 'ROUND! (Point up and circle hand.) JESUS CARES! **KIDS AND LEADERS:** (Point up.) JESUS CARES, (Circle hand.) NOW AND FOREVER!

Divide the kids into four teams and have each team line up behind a hay bale (cone).

SAY: **Sheep are not good listeners. Sometimes they walk away from their shepherd and try to go their own way. We need to keep these sheep together as a flock. Can you pretend to be a shepherd and herd a sheep? A sheep wants to get away, but you need to be a shepherd and guide the sheep back to its pen.**

Demonstrate the relay as you explain each step. **When I say, "Go!" the first person will use this sheep herding tool** (fly swatter) **to guide the sheep** (white balloon). **The sheep is getting away, so you need to gently push the sheep down to the hay bale** (cone), **go around and behind it, and then come back to the front of the line, the same place you started from. Then it will be someone else's turn to go. Hand the herding tool to the next person in line so he or she can train to be a shepherd. Then go to the end of the line and sit down.**

Answer any questions, and then complete the relay. Keep the extra balloons nearby to replace balloons that pop. When finished, have the students sit together with their team. **SAY: Did the sheep always go the direction you wanted them to go? Was it frustrating?** (Let students answer.) **Jesus tells us that His sheep know His voice and listen. Sometimes we listen to our Good Shepherd and go where He leads, and sometimes we don't. But Jesus always loves us and cares for us, and He leads us to everlasting life with Him.**

Fun in the Play Yard

If your Games time is in a play yard, consider using activities from the Learning Area too. Caring for Sheep is a possibility.

Or play Barnyard Mix-up. In advance, mark your playing area with cones so the children know the boundaries. No other materials are needed.

Explain that you will tell the children to pretend to be an animal. You will whisper the name of the animal in their ear. When you say "Go!" they will start acting like the animal by making that animal's noise and by moving like that animal. Their job is to find all the other animals that are the same, and stand together as a group, or herd. The game is over when all of the mixed up animals are sorted into groups.

Start by assigning only two animals, but work up to three or four. Possible animal options include cows, horses, pigs, chickens, sheep, roosters, cats, dogs, and mice. After the game, **SAY: Sometimes we are mixed up and go the wrong way. But Jesus loves us and gathers us together!**

Closing

🕐 **about 15 minutes**

Closing Puppet Skit

You need: *Polly the Pig Puppet*, Puppet Script, *Lesson 1 Little Sprouts Early Childhood Leaflet*, *Lesson 1 My Shepherd Collectible*, and children's take-home items

Seat the children on the floor or carpet squares. **SING:** "My Shepherd" (*Leader CD* Track 17). Bring out the *Polly the Pig Puppet* to talk about how we can tell Jesus cares for us. Use the Puppet Script from the *Leader CD.*

After the skit, close with this echo prayer: **Dear Jesus, / thank You for being with us / at *Barnyard Roundup* today. / Thank You / that You care for us now / and forever. / Help us trust You always. / In Your name we pray. Amen.**

SAY: Let's meet again at *Barnyard Roundup!* Next time, we'll hear how Jesus took care of a lot of people. It's great to know He provides for our needs—what we need to live here on earth, and what we need so we'll live forever with Jesus. **SAY:** GATHER 'ROUND! (Point up and circle hand.) **JESUS CARES! KIDS AND LEADERS:** (Point up.) **JESUS CARES,** (Circle hand.) **NOW AND FOREVER!** Now let's do it again in a whisper voice. (Repeat Take-Home Point.) **Now let's do it in our loudest voice.** (Repeat Take-Home Point.)

Show a Lesson 1 lesson leaflet. **SAY: Please take this home and ask your Mom or Dad to read it. There is something special on the front and back pages for your family to do together.**

Thank your Helpers. Send home *Lesson 1 Little Sprouts Early Childhood Leaflet*, the *Lesson 1 My Shepherd Collectible*, and other take-home items. As you say good-bye to children at sign-out time, remind parents to read the leaflet at home.

Looking Ahead

Pray for your students and Helpers.

Restock or prepare learning areas with Lesson 2 materials.

Lay out *Poster Fun* from *Little Sprouts Early Childhood Leaflets* for the next lesson's transition activity.

Prepare the Storytelling materials.

Review the next lesson's plans. Ask your team members what adjustments might improve the schedule or activities.

Roundup Leader Devotion

Bible Story: Jesus Feeds 5,000 People
Mark 6:30–44; John 6:1–14

Bible Memory Verse:
"He makes me lie down in green pastures." Psalm 23:2

Read Mark 6:30–44 and John 6:1–44 and
Think on These Things:

You may be wondering why there are two Bible accounts of the same story for this lesson! First, the miracle of the feeding of the 5,000 people is told in all four Gospels: Matthew, Mark, Luke, and John! They are all the same, and they are all different. Mark's Gospel account compares the people to sheep who need a shepherd in verse 34. The John account includes the reference to the boy whose lunch was the source of the five loaves and two fish used by Jesus.

Mark 6:30–34 Jesus took his disciples away from the crowds to a desolate place to rest, but a large crowd followed them. A tired Jesus "had compassion on them, because they were like sheep without a shepherd" (v. 34). So, in that desolate place where green grass grew, He provided spiritual nourishment to those "sheep" with His teaching.

Mark 6:35–38 Jesus provides also for our physical needs. In the story, it was late, everyone was hungry, and the disciples thought it would be a good time to send everyone home. Jesus told the disciples to give the crowd something to eat. They responded that it was an expensive and impossible task to satisfy so many. At His request, they identified the sum total of the food resources: five barley loaves and two fish.

Mark 6:39–41 Then Jesus, the Good Shepherd who provides for His sheep, acted. He told the people to sit down on the green grass. He looked up to heaven and gave thanks to His Father and divided up the five loaves and fish among them all.

Mark 6:42–44 Jesus, our Good Shepherd, provided "green pastures" for those "sheep." The five thousand men, plus the women and children with them, ate and were full—with twelve baskets of leftovers!

Jesus, our Good Shepherd, provides "green pastures" for us, His "sheep." Each day as His flock, we lay our needs of body and soul before Him, and He has compassion on us. He provides for our physical needs daily and richly. He provides for our spiritual needs—forgiveness of sins, life, and salvation—through the teaching of His Word and the gifts of the Sacraments.

Help your students to see the bounty with which God provides for all of our needs in the everyday miracles we take for granted, and ask Him to forgive us for forgetting to thank Him for His care.

Take-Home Point:
Jesus provides, now and forever!

Kids need to know that Jesus provides for all their needs. He has promised to answer prayer—and He does! When obstacles threaten to dishearten us, we can trust Jesus to provide. Jesus is always ready to care and provide for us. He is never too tired, too busy, or without resources. Jesus gave thanks to His Father in heaven. He gives us what we need now and what we truly need most: eternal life in heaven.

Because of sin in the world, it's sometimes difficult to get the things we need and we don't trust Jesus to give us all good things. Still, Jesus, our Good Shepherd, abundantly provides all that we need for our bodies and our souls.

Jesus Gathers Us Together: Jesus gathers us all together in His flock, the Church, to provide for us. Through the power of the Holy Spirit, we know our caring Jesus, trust in Him to provide for all our needs, and give thanks to Him for His abundant provision of "green pastures," now and forever.

Prayer: Dear Jesus, forgive us when we don't trust You to provide for us. Thank You for all the good gifts You give us here in this life. Thank You for abundantly providing what we need most of all: forgiveness, life, and salvation. In Your name we pray. Amen.

Lesson 2
Jesus Feeds 5,000 People

Mark 6:30–44; John 6:1–14

Today You Need

Leader and Student Materials (p. 10)

Every Lesson Supplies (p. 11)

Learning Area Supplies: plastic tub; green paper; scissors; green Easter grass or green ribbon (optional); 2–3 small blankets; paper plates; many construction-paper cutouts of fish and bread (save for Storytelling supplies); baskets

Storytelling Supplies: 3 small (5-inch) paper plates with Jesus, Disciples, and Boy figures glued on them; wooden craft sticks; construction-paper fish (4) and bread loaves (10); dry beans or rice; tape; 2 beanbags or soft balls (optional)

See the Master Supply List on *Leader CD* for complete list for all lessons.

Welcome, *Poster Fun*, and Learning Areas

 **20 minutes**

Play music from the *Leader CD* in the background. Have Helpers with nametags stationed inside and outside of the entrance to greet and direct families to the welcome table. While helping children with nametags and attendance stickers, ask the parents/caregivers to use the *Sign In & Out Sheet* each day. Have the children put their sheep in the sheep pen to take attendance.

SAY: Hi, I'm (Leader's name). (Child's name), **welcome to** *Barnyard Roundup*! **We'll do so many fun activities here. We'll learn more about Jesus and His love for us. We'll hear how He is with us, providing for us and protecting us. You can go to the** *Poster Fun* **table. The Helpers will give you the posters and directions.**

Poster Fun Helpers give out posters and directions. Make sure first and last names are printed on the posters. Remind parents to leave the posters on the table before moving to the next activity. Helpers gather and sort posters alphabetically by last name to prepare for Lesson 3.

Poster Fun for Parents and Kids

You need: your child's *Poster Fun*, green crayon, and *Basket Sticker*

Parents: Make sure you have the same *Poster Fun* your child started last time. Look at the picture on the front with your child. **SAY: This picture reminds me of the fun you had at** *Barnyard Roundup* **last time. What animal got a name?** (The pig, Polly)

Turn the poster over to the back page. Have your child repeat the Lesson 2 Bible Memory Verse after you. Point to the Lesson 2 shepherd staff icon and **SAY: Shepherds use this special tool to keep sheep from wandering away from the shepherd who cares for them. Jesus cares for us! Color the staff green.**

Open *Poster Fun* and point to the Lesson 2 picture. **SAY: I see a green pasture just like the pastures where good shepherds take their sheep to eat. But who is this?** (Jesus) **It looks like He is supposed to be holding something in His hands.**

Give your child the *Basket Sticker*. Help him or her affix it to Jesus' hands on Picture 2. **SAY: The sheep were led to green grass by the shepherd. In today's Bible story, Jesus fed a crowd sitting on the grass. Repeat after me: JESUS PROVIDES, NOW AND FOREVER.**

Leave the leaflet on the table. Take your child to Learning Area 1. Once your child is engaged in the activity, you may quietly leave.

Transition Activities

Learning Area 1: Make It
Green Grass Clipping

Goal: Children will exercise their small muscles by snipping green grass.

You Need: shallow plastic tub (such as an under-bed storage container); green paper (various types); scissors; green Easter grass or green ribbon (optional)

Put green paper in the tub. Different types of paper will add interest to the activity: crepe paper, tissue paper, wrapping paper, and construction paper. Precut strips of the paper to two to three inches wide. You could also include green Easter grass or two- to three-foot pieces of green ribbon.

SAY: Last time, where did the Good Shepherd take His sheep to eat? (Green pastures) **Pastures are fields of grass. In our Bible story, we will hear about some people who sat on some green grass to eat their lunch. What do you call it when you eat outside on the grass?** (A picnic!) **But this was a very special picnic. Jesus gave a huge crowd of people their food. We are going to use this paper to make some green grass. Can you cut the paper into little pieces?**

Assist children as necessary. Some might have enough control to make a fringe on a strip of paper. Others will simply snip it into little pieces. Save the green grass to use with Lesson 4.

Learning Area Options:

Bible Story Coloring Page (*Leader CD*): Helpers can encourage the children to identify objects and people on the Coloring Page. Then they can tell the children that they will be hearing this Bible story a little later. The children could take a strip of green paper and fringe it like grass, then glue it onto the bottom of the Coloring Page.

Learning Area 2: Imagine It
Get in Your Group

Goal: The children will practice getting into groups of two to five.

You Need: nothing

SAY: In our Bible story, Jesus told His disciples to have the people sit in groups to be fed. Today, we will imagine we are getting in a group to have our special food from Jesus! Using children or Helpers, demonstrate what a group of two people looks like. Then show three-, four-, and five-person groups. **I need everyone to walk around. When I say, JESUS PROVIDES, everyone will stop. Then I will say a number. You have to find enough friends to help you make a group of that size. When you have made your group, sit down.** When all groups have been formed and are seated, lead the entire group in the take-home point: **SAY**: GATHER 'ROUND! (Point up and circle hand.) **JESUS PROVIDES! KIDS AND LEADERS:** (Point up.) **JESUS PROVIDES,** (Circle hand.) **NOW AND FOREVER!** Repeat as time and interest permit. Some of the youngest children may have trouble with this, so be sure to encourage older ones to help them with counting or finding a friend. If your group is large enough, when you repeat the activity, **SAY: This time, you have to be in a group with different friends.**

Learning Area 3: Act It Out
Eating on the Green Grass

Goal: The children will act out being on a picnic, eating fish and bread.

You Need: 2–3 small blankets or tablecloths; paper plates; many construction-paper cutouts of fish and bread; 1 basket for each blanket

Set out the blankets or tablecloths, more or fewer depending upon the size of your group. Designate one child to be the "disciple" for each blanket. Divide the other children up equally to sit on the blankets.

SAY: Have you ever been on a picnic? Accept answers. **What if you went on a picnic and didn't bring any food! Would it still be a picnic?** (No) **In our Bible story today, we will hear about some people who went out to see Jesus. They wanted to hear Him tell about God's love. But they stayed so long that it was time to eat and they didn't have any food!**

SAY: Jesus fed them in a special way, which we will hear about later. But for now, we are going to pretend that we have just been listening to Jesus, and now His helpers are giving us some food. Pass out one plate to each child, then have the "disciples" pass out the bread and fish equally. Remind the children to use good manners and say "please" and "thank you." The children can pretend to heartily eat their food.

SAY: Do you think Jesus would give them food that tasted bad? I'm sure it was delicious. Have the "disciples" pick up all the leftovers and put them in baskets. **We ate so much we are full! Rub your tummies to show you are full. Jesus provides for us— everything we need!** Let the other children have a turn to pass out the food.

Opening

🕐 **20 minutes**

You Need: altar, Lyrics Sheets, Puppet Scripts and props, *Polly the Pig Puppet*, bell, Bible

Ring the bell to get everyone's attention. **SING** (to the tune of *"The Farmer in the Dell"*):

> It's Bible story time. It's Bible story time.
> We're going to hear how Jesus provides.
> It's Bible story time.

Repeat as needed, encouraging the children to sing along as they move toward the altar area and are seated.

SAY: I am so happy to see you again today at our *Barnyard Roundup*. Who can tell me something you learned about the Good Shepherd? Accept a few answers. **Today, we will hear about a time when Jesus gave people some food to eat. We know this really happened because it is in God's book, the Bible.** Hold up the Bible.

Show the children how to fold their hands. **SAY: In the name of the Father and of the Son and of the Holy Spirit. Amen. We say those words to remember that God is with us. Now I am going to light the candle to remind us that Jesus is the Light. The sun shines every day, and Jesus shines on us every day!** Light the candle.

SING: "I Am Jesus' Little Lamb" (*Leader CD* Track 15), using the actions from the Lesson 1 Opening, or "All Together Come and Gather" (*Leader CD* Track 2).

Teach the Take-Home Point

SAY: Jesus is our Good Shepherd. Today, we'll see how He provides for us. What do you think the word *provides* means? (Give the children time to explain and give examples. Jesus gives us everything we need. In our last lesson, we talked about the care and protection He provides. Parents give us food and clothing and a home. Parents plan ahead for taking you places or they plan special events like birthday parties. Teachers provide supplies for art projects. They prepare what needs to be done before you arrive.) **Jesus thinks through every detail of what you need! He doesn't forget anything that needs to be done. He provides for us abundantly! He gives us what we need to live now, and He has taken care of what we need in order to live with Him forever in heaven.**

SAY: Here at *Barnyard Roundup*, we have a special way of reminding one another of how God has gathered us together to be His children. Let's stand up. When you hear me or one of the Helpers say "GATHER 'ROUND! JESUS PROVIDES!" while pointing up and making a circle with our hand like this (Demonstrate), **then you will all say "JESUS PROVIDES, NOW AND FOREVER!" while doing the same motion. Let's try it. Are you ready?**

SAY: GATHER 'ROUND! (Point up and circle hand.) **JESUS PROVIDES! KIDS AND LEADERS:** (Point up.) **JESUS PROVIDES,** (Circle hand.) **NOW AND FOREVER! Now let's do it again in a whisper voice.** Repeat Take-Home Point. **Now let's do it in our loudest voice.** Repeat Take-Home Point.

Pray

Have children sit down. **SAY: Now let's talk to God by praying.** Invite the children to fold their hands, bow their heads, and repeat each phrase of the prayer after you. **SAY: Dear Lord Jesus, / You give us everything we need. / Help us to listen / and learn / how much You provide for us. / We trust in You, Jesus. / Amen.**

Opening Puppet Skit

You Need: *Polly the Pig Puppet*, Puppet Script (*Leader CD*)

Polly is worried that the farmer will forget to feed her.

After the skit, **SAY: Do you ever get hungry like Polly?** Accept answers. **We all get hungry; we need food to stay healthy and have energy. God knows that we need food because He made us that way! Let's listen to our Bible story now and hear how He took care of a large group of people.**

Bible Storytelling

🕐 **20 minutes**

(handwritten: YES Don't need three people)

You Need: *Leader CD*; 3 small (5-inch) paper plates; Lesson 2 Coloring Page (*Leader CD*); glue; scissors; wooden craft sticks or tongue depressors

Cut out the following figures from the Coloring Page: Jesus, Disciples, Boy. Glue them onto the plates. Attach wooden crafts sticks to the plates for use as puppets.

SAY: Jesus and His helpers (Hold up plates with Jesus and Disciples.) **were very tired. They had been telling a lot of people about God's love.** (Turn Jesus toward Disciples as if talking.) **Jesus said "Let's go somewhere that is quiet so we can rest for a while."** So they went on a boat across the lake. (Move Jesus and Disciples from left to right in front of you.) **But when they got there, guess what! The people had found out where they were going and made it there first! So when they got out of the boat, they saw all the people.** (Put down plates and do the following chant, encouraging the children to join you. Use the same refrain repeatedly throughout the story.)

(handwritten: Cute)

> **One thousand** (*Hold up index finger.*)
> **Two thousand** (*Hold up middle finger to show 2.*)
> **Three thousand** (*Hold up ring finger to show 3.*)
> **Four!** (*Hold up pinkie finger to show 4.*)
> **Five thousand men** (*Hold up thumb to show 5.*)
> **And even more!** (*Clap on the word "more."*)

SAY: Jesus could have said, "Leave Me alone. I'm tired." But instead, the Bible tells us He looked at them like a good shepherd looks at his sheep. He felt sorry for them and wanted to help them. So He began to teach them many things about God's love. (Hold up Jesus paper-plate puppet and move slightly as if talking.) **He talked all morning, and He talked all afternoon, and the people were so happy to listen to Him that they stayed all day.**

(Hold up Disciples paper-plate puppet. Have them look toward Jesus puppet.) **Finally, Jesus' helpers said to Him, "We are far away from any towns, and the people are hungry. We need to send them away so they can get some food."** (Slightly move Jesus as if He is talking.) **But Jesus said, "You give them something to eat." Jesus' helpers said, "Even if we had a lot of money, we could not feed all of these people! Can't You see that there are . . . "**

Put down plates and repeat the chanted refrain.

Hold up the Boy puppet and the Disciples puppet.

SAY: A boy came to the helpers and said, "I can share

my lunch. I have five loaves of bread and two fish." The disciples took him to Jesus, but they said, "This is not enough; don't you realize there are . . . "

Put down plates and repeat the chanted refrain.

(Pick up Jesus puppet.) **SAY: Jesus said, "Tell the people to sit down on the green grass in groups." Then He took the boy's lunch and looked up to heaven and thanked God. He broke the bread in pieces and gave it to the helpers. They passed out the food to the people, and everyone had enough.** (Move Disciples around two or three times distributing bread and fish.) **It was a miracle—something so special and powerful only God can do!**

Put down plates and repeat the chanted refrain.

SAY: The people were so full! Jesus did not just give them a little bit of food; He gave them a lot. There was even extra food that no one had eaten! Then Jesus told His disciples to take some baskets and pick up all the leftovers. So they went to the . . .

Put down plates and repeat the chanted refrain.

SAY: There were twelve baskets full of leftovers! The people were so amazed at how Jesus had fed them. I love this story! It reminds me of how Jesus provides everything we need. Let's say our Take-Home Point before going to our next activities. SAY: GATHER 'ROUND! (Point up and circle hand.) **JESUS PROVIDES! KIDS AND LEADERS:** (Point up.) **JESUS PROVIDES,** (Circle hand.) **NOW AND FOREVER!**

Rotation Sites

🕐 **1 hour**

Early Childhood Teams get into three Rotation Groups. Each Rotation Group moves to their assigned Rotation Site. When it is time to move to a different Rotation Site, ring a bell three times.

Rotation 1: Bible Story Application

🕐 **About 20 minutes**

Review

You need: *Lesson 2 Little Sprouts Early Childhood Leaflet* and stickers, crayons

Give *Lesson 2 Little Sprouts Early Childhood Leaflets* to small-group Leaders. Sit at tables or on carpet squares in a circle on the floor. Make sure each child's name gets on his or her leaflet. As you pass out each one, **SAY: This is for Jesus' little lamb** (name of child). When all the leaflets are distributed, **SAY: Point to your name. Who knows your name? Jesus, the Good Shepherd, knows your name! You are one of His precious sheep. He'll always provide what you need.**

SAY: Look at the picture. Look at all the people. Do you remember how many people there were? (Five thousand men and even more!)

SAY: Where are the people sitting? (On the grass and on rocks) **Point to the grass. This grass is green just like the pasture where the good shepherd took his sheep to eat. And now Jesus, the Good Shepherd, is feeding these people on the green grass. But will they eat grass?** (No) **Point to the little boy. Can you remember how much food he shared?** (Five loaves of bread and two fish)

SAY: What do you think the people said to Jesus after He fed them? (I hope they said thank You.) **Jesus said thank You to God before He passed out the food. We say thank You to God when we pray before we eat. Now let's look inside.**

Leaflet Activity

Pass out the stickers for Lesson 2.

SAY: Where do you think these children are? (A park) **What color do you think the grass should be?** (Yes, let's color the grass green.) Allow time for children to color the grass. **When Jesus got off the boat and saw all the people, He felt sorry for them because they were like sheep who needed a shepherd. Look at the playground picture. See if there's anyone who needs help. Point to someone who needs help.**

Accept answers as you discuss the following scenarios, in any order. **SAY: Oh no, I see some children who are fighting. What do they need?** (Yes, they need someone to help them stop fighting. Then they should say "I'm sorry" and forgive each other.) **Do you see a sticker that reminds us of how God forgives us? Let's put the cross sticker by these children to help them remember that God forgives them because Jesus died on the cross to take their sins away. Now they can forgive each other.** (Children place the *Cross Sticker* near the fighting children).

SAY: This child sees a boy who is eating a snack. I wonder why he is sad? (He is hungry.) **Let's look at our stickers and find one that will help this boy. Could one of the other children share a snack with him? Put the lunch bag sticker near the hungry boy.** (Children place the *Food Sticker* near the hungry child).

SAY: What do you notice about the girl at the top of the slide? (She looks cold.) **Let's look at our stickers. Do you see something that would help her to feel better?** (Yes, a jacket.) **Do you think her mother sees that's she's cold and brings her jacket? Let's put the jacket sticker by her.** (Children place the *Jacket Sticker* on or near the cold child).

SAY: Jesus cares about us right now. When we are hurt or sad, He can help us. He provides that help in many ways through our parents, family, and friends. But Jesus also cares about our future. He grants us forgiveness of our sins so we can be with Him in heaven, where we will never be sad or hurt ever again.

Encourage the children to finish coloring the picture as time and interest permit.

SAY: GATHER 'ROUND! (Point up and circle hand.) **JESUS PROVIDES! KIDS AND LEADERS:** (Point up.) **JESUS PROVIDES,** (Circle hand.) **NOW AND FOREVER!**

SING: "We Plow the Fields and Scatter" (*Leader CD* Track 19).

Rotation 2: Bible Challenge

🕐 **About 20 minutes**

The Bible Memory Song

You need: Bible with the Bible Memory Verse marked, *Bible Memory Songs Sign Chart*, *Leader CD*, and CD player

SAY: Our Bible Memory Verse is "He makes me lie down in green pastures," Psalm 23:2. Those words are from God's book, the Bible. Let's sing this Bible Memory Verse together. Play *Leader CD* Track 10. Add the motions as shown on the *Bible Memory Songs Sign Chart*, from the *Leader CD*.

Story Review

You need: 7 beanbags (2 for fish and 5 for bread) or create 2 fish and 5 bread loaves from construction paper, dry beans or rice, tape, and a stapler

Before the children arrive, cut four fish shapes from green construction paper and 10 bread loaves from brown construction paper. Staple and tape two similar shapes together, leaving an opening at the top. Pour some dry beans or rice into the fish and bread and seal them tightly with more tape.

SAY: When Jesus gave the food to the people, they had to pass it around and share it. We will pretend to pass the food around our circle by using these bread and fish shapes.

Form a circle. Spread out your Helpers throughout the circle to help the children with passing the "food." Spend some time letting the children practice passing the bread and fish. Pass the fish one way and the bread another. When you feel the children are ready,

SAY: Now we are going to say a rhyme while we pass around our bread and fish. Let's practice our rhyme first:

> Pass the fish. Pass the bread.
> Make sure everyone gets fed.

Practice until the children are comfortable with the rhyme. **SAY:** Now we will do the rhyme *while* we pass the bread and fish. At the end of the rhyme, when we say the word "fed," if you are holding the bread or fish, hold it up high. Then we will all say, "Thank You, Jesus, thank You!" Each time, we'll remember how Jesus provides for us. Repeat as time permits.

Sharing Circle Game

You need: 2 fish (simple outline cut from green construction paper) and 5 bread loaves (ovals cut from brown construction paper)

Arrange the children in a circle. Choose one child to be Jesus' disciple and sit in the middle of the circle. Explain that you will pretend to be Jesus. They will pretend to be people in the crowd. To play the game, they will need to have their hands behind their backs. Demonstrate. One of them will be chosen to be the child with the two fish and five loaves of bread.

Each round of the game, start by having all the children close their eyes and cover their eyes with their hands. Place the loaves and fishes behind one child's back and have the child hide it in his or her hands. Instruct all the children (the crowd) to place their hands behind their backs and open their eyes.

As Jesus, you (or your Helper) will ask your disciple in the middle to find food for the crowd. Have the disciple point to a child around the circle (someone in the crowd). **SING** (chant) (to the tune of "Who Stole the Cookie from the Cookie Jar?"):

> **Who has some supper for the crowd today?**
> **Does** (name of child) **have some supper for the crowd today?**
> **Who, me?** (Child in crowd echoes the question.)
> **Yes, you!**
> **Couldn't be.** (Child in crowd echoes the phrase.)
> **Then who?**

Let the disciple in the middle point to another child and repeat. When the disciple finds the child with the food (the child sings "Could be"), have Jesus (you or a Helper) take the food, hold it up in the air, look to heaven and **SING** (chant) (to the same tune):

> **Thank You, thank You, Father for this food to-day.** (Children echo.)
> **Please bless** (Children echo.)
> **This food.**
> **Give food** (Children echo.)
> **To all!**

Play more rounds by choosing different children to become the disciple in the middle who guesses which child has food. To make the game go faster for larger groups, let the disciple have only one turn.

Rotation 3: Crafts

First from Playdough

◷ **20 minutes**

Jesus Fish Sand Art

You Need

- *Jesus Fish Sand Art* board, 1 per person
- Paper clips or toothpicks
- Spoons
- *Rainbow Craft Sand* (sold separately)
- Containers to hold and catch sand, 1 per color
- Embellishments
- Picture hanger or magnet, 1 per student (optional)
- Tape or glue (optional)
- Sandwich zipper bags
- Finished sample craft

Make It!

Gather supplies. Leaders put the child's name on the back of the board. Show children the supplies.

Use a paper clip or toothpick to pull up an edge of a section of the sand-art board, exposing the sticky die-cut shape. The children should start in the center and work out, one section at a time. Model, and then help and encourage individuals as needed.

Direct the children to hold the board over a container to catch excess sand.

Children spoon sand onto the revealed adhesive section. Encourage them to start with darker sand first. Children can use more than one color in an area or add other decorations.

Children continue to pull off pieces and apply colored sand until the entire board is covered.

Leaders tape or glue a picture hanger or magnet to the back.

Children put the fish in a sandwich bag for the ride home. Help the children seal it tightly.

Putting It All Together

SAY: Jesus provided food for thousands of hungry people by making lots of fish from the two little fish in a boy's lunch. Through this miracle, Jesus showed that He is true God, and that He loves us and is able to take care of us. But Jesus provided more than just food that day. He provided for the people's spiritual needs too, teaching them about God and His love for them.

As you work on your fish sand art, remember that Jesus loves you and provides for you too. He leads you in green pastures, providing what you need to live now. But more, He has taken care of what you need in order to live with Him forever in heaven: He is the Good Shepherd who laid down His life for you.

When you look at your sand-art fish, thank Jesus for providing what you need. Or give your fish to someone who needs to hear about Jesus. Share the Bible story of how Jesus provides, now and forever!

SAY: GATHER 'ROUND! (Point up and circle hand.) JESUS PROVIDES! **KIDS AND LEADERS:** (Point up.) **JESUS PROVIDES,** (Circle hand.) **NOW AND FOREVER!**

Gather a Great Idea!

For additional ideas like *I Am Jesus' Little Lamb Necklace,* see the Bonus Crafts in the *Craft Leader Guide.*

Snack

⏱ **20 minutes**

Baskets of Blessings

You Need

- A plate for each child
- A wooden craft stick for each child
- A cupcake for each child
- Half of a licorice braid for each child
- 5 pieces of graham cereal (e.g., Golden Grahams) for each child
- 2 fish-shaped crackers for each child, any flavor
- A bowl of frosting for each table
- A finished example
- Hand sanitizer & napkins
- Cups & water

Advance Preparation

Divide frosting among bowls for each table. Before the children arrive, put all items listed above on each Team's table.

When Kids Arrive

Take the children to the restroom. Have them wash their hands. Have them sit in their places.

SAY: Let's make a snack to help us remember that Jesus abundantly provides for us, saves us, and protects us—now and forever! This snack will remind you of the miracle Jesus provided.

SAY: Let's start by saying the Bible verse: "He makes me lie down in green pastures," Psalm 23:2. Jesus provides for us like shepherds provide for sheep. Remember that sheep like to be in a group, follow one another, and follow their shepherd. It's the shepherd's job to lead them to water and food like you find in green pastures. Sheep love to eat green things! They eat grass, clover, and other green plants growing in pastures. Sheep spend about seven hours a day eating! That's a lot of food!

SAY: The Bible story is also about a lot of food. Jesus' miracle provided food for over five thousand people to eat. Jesus provides food for us too!

Making the Snack

Hold up the finished example. **SAY:** We're going to make a basket of blessings.

Demonstrate step by step as you explain how to make the basket. Work together as a class, one step at a time, until each child has completed the same step, and then go on at the same time.

- Give each child a plate with a cupcake on it, a wooden craft stick, and a napkin. Children use their stick to spread frosting on their cupcake.

- Children add the basket handles. Children use the craft stick to poke two small holes on opposite sides of the cupcake's top. Leaders assist as needed. Pass out the licorice. Children put one end of the licorice into each hole.

- Children add the food into the basket. Leaders pass out the cereal and fish crackers. Children set five pieces of cereal and two fish crackers in the frosting.

SAY: This looks like the basket of food the boy had in our Bible story! Jesus provided for the entire crowd of people with the bread and fish. Jesus provides all *we* need, now and forever! Say a snack prayer and eat.

Before They Go

SAY: GATHER 'ROUND! (Point up and circle hand.) JESUS PROVIDES! **KIDS AND LEADERS:** (Point up.) JESUS PROVIDES, (Circle hand.) NOW AND FOREVER! **SAY:** Shepherds lead sheep to green pastures, where they graze until they are full. Jesus fills us up as He provides for us through our parents, family, and friends. And we are filled up with God's Word, where we learn about Jesus, our Savior.

Games

🕐 **20 minutes**

Fly the Coop

You Need

- ▪ Lots of water balloons and containers to hold them
- ▪ 6 or more crates or buckets, depending on group size
- ▪ Chicken coop graphic (*Director CD*), scissors, and tape

Get Ready

Fill the water balloons. This game calls for a good number of water balloons. It will be important to have an even amount of balloons for each team.

Tape chicken coop printouts to buckets.

Here We Go

SAY: Howdy, farmers! Welcome back to Bales of Fun Games! In today's Bible lesson, we hear when Jesus provided for His followers by taking a small amount of fish and bread and multiplying it to feed thousands of people. Jesus promises to provide for us too.

Divide the children into groups of two or three. Give each pair or trio a chicken coop (bucket/crate). Encourage them to spread out, find their own space, and have each child hold onto a part of the coop.

SAY: Farmers provide for their animals too—food, water, shelter, and more. We're going to pretend to be farmers and play a game called Fly the Coop. A coop is a henhouse or pen made just for chickens. But your chickens have flown the coop. Your Team needs to get them all back! I will call out one Team at a time to get ready to catch a chicken. A chicken (water balloon) **will be thrown into the air, like it's flying. As a Team, keep holding onto the coop (bucket) together and move and catch the chicken in your coop. Only one Team at a time will catch the chicken. Everyone else must stay in their spot.**

Have an adult volunteer with a good arm throw the water balloons one at a time to each Team. To make it less challenging, toss the balloons underhand. To make it more challenging, toss overhand.

It will be important to have only one Team moving at a time, as the kids will be looking up at the balloons, not around at one another. Make sure you throw an even amount of balloons to each Team. Have the students help you pick up the balloon pieces (feathers) when

the game is over. After every Team has had several turns, have them sit on the ground. **SAY: As a farmer, you provided for those chickens by giving them a home, the coop. It is often easy to remember that Jesus provides for us food and a house to live in, but what about the things we can't see? Can you think of the spiritual things that Jesus gives us each day?** (Love, forgiveness, grace, mercy) **Most important, Jesus provided Himself by dying on the cross and rising again to give us life everlasting. So let's say it together. SAY: GATHER 'ROUND!** (Point up and circle hand.) **JESUS PROVIDES! KIDS AND LEADERS:** (Point up.) **JESUS PROVIDES,** (Circle hand.) **NOW AND FOREVER!**

Fun in the Play Yard

If your Games time is in a play yard, consider using activities from the Learning Area too. Get In Your Group is a possibility.

Or play Pig Out! In advance, set up a cone for each relay group to stand behind. About twenty feet away from the cones, set up a table.

Explain that each Team will stand behind a cone and pretend to be pigs. A Leader will pretend to be a farmer and call the first person in line to come for dinner. That child will race down to the table. Designate a Team Leader or volunteer to place a dish of Jell-o out for each child. Keeping their hands behind their backs, the children (pigs) must eat some of the Jell-o and race back to the cone. After everyone has had a turn, **SAY: Farmers provide food for their animals. Jesus provides not only food for us but also all that we need, including eternal life!**

Closing

🕐 **about 20 minutes**

Closing Puppet Skit

You need: *Polly the Pig Puppet*, Puppet Script, *Lesson 2 Little Sprouts Early Childhood Leaflet*, *Lesson 2 My Shepherd Collectible*, and children's take-home items

Seat the children on the floor or carpet squares. **SING:** "My Shepherd" (*Leader CD* Track 17). Bring out the *Polly the Pig Puppet* to talk about how we know Jesus provides for us. Use the Puppet Script from the *Leader CD*.

After the skit, close with this echo prayer: **Dear Jesus, / thank You for being with us / at *Barnyard Roundup* today. / Help us to remember / that You provide for us / now and forever. / Help us trust You always. / In Your name we pray. Amen.**

SAY: Let's meet again at *Barnyard Roundup*! Next time, we'll hear another story Jesus told people about how He gives them what they need. It's great to grow in God's Word! **SAY: GATHER 'ROUND!** (Point up and circle hand.) **JESUS PROVIDES! KIDS AND LEADERS:** (Point up.) **JESUS PROVIDES,** (Circle hand.) **NOW AND FOREVER! Now let's do it again in a whisper voice.** (Repeat Take-Home Point.) **Now let's do it in our loudest voice.** (Repeat Take-Home Point.)

Show a lesson leaflet. **SAY: Please take this home and ask your Mom or Dad to read it. There is something special on the front and back page for your family to do together.**

Thank your Helpers. Send home *Lesson 2 Little Sprouts Early Childhood Leaflet*, *Lesson 2 My Shepherd Collectible*, and other take-home items. As you say good-bye to children at sign-out time, remind parents to read the leaflet at home.

Looking Ahead

Pray for your students and Helpers.

Restock or prepare Learning Area with Lesson 3 materials.

Lay out *Poster Fun* from *Little Sprouts Early Childhood Leaflets* for the next lesson's transition activity.

Prepare the Storytelling materials. Prepare a container of hardened mud for the Bible story.

Review the next lesson's plans. Ask your team members what adjustments might improve the schedule or activities.

Lesson 3
Roundup Leader Devotion
Bible Story: Jesus Tells about a Sower
Matthew 13:1–23

Bible Memory Verse:
"He leads me in paths of righteousness." Psalm 23:3

Read Matthew 13:1–23 and
Think on These Things:

This parable was told at the Sea of Galilee from a boat. Jesus taught many things by telling parables. A parable is an earthly story with a heavenly meaning. This parable shows the sower faithfully sowing the seed and trusting God to provide the harvest.

Matthew 13:1–9 The sight of a farmer sowing seed was familiar to Jesus' listeners. The farmer would sow the seed by hand. He'd reach his hands into a seed pouch he carried at his waist and scatter the seed over the ground. In the parable of the sower, the farmer is generous with the seed and tosses it out everywhere! The seed falls on the path, on rocky ground, among thorns, and on good soil. Jesus says the seed is the Word of God.

Matthew 13:10–17 When questioned by His disciples, Jesus lets them know they are blessed to see with their eyes and hear with their ears the Gospel message He is proclaiming.

Matthew 13:18–23 Here, Jesus explains the problems with three of the soils and how the evil one, tribulation or persecution, or cares of the world destroy a fruitful harvest. But Jesus encourages His disciples with the good soil that produces a bountiful and abundant harvest by God's gracious and merciful hand.

As VBS Leaders, we are blessed to be used by God to sow His Word on the children in our care. We don't always know what the soil is like. And plants take time to grow, so we may never see what is produced. But that's not our row to hoe. God says, "My Word . . . shall not return to Me empty, but it shall accomplish that which I purpose, and shall succeed in the thing for which I sent it" (Isaiah 55:11). Through us, Jesus is sowing the seed out of the abundance of God's love that is already in our hearts, trusting that He will provide the harvest.

Take-Home Point:
Jesus leads, now and forever!

Kid's ears hear lots of messages in this world. Many of the messages direct the children to their own efforts and their own or the world's version of truth rather than learning from God's true and Holy Word.

Jesus Gathers Us Together: Our hearts are sinful, so we don't want to listen to or receive God's Word; but Jesus, our Good Shepherd, works through God's Word, gives us faith and ears to hear, protects us from Satan, and leads us in the paths of righteousness. He does this right now and leads us to eternal life and salvation through the seed of God's Word. Like the farmer who

scattered the seed everywhere, God abundantly spreads His Word and provides the abundant and fruitful harvest. We do not grow weary in sharing Jesus' love.

Prayer: Dear Jesus, thank You for leading us in the path of righteousness. Thank You for giving us faith by the Holy Spirit to believe that You died and rose again for us. Forgive us for the times we let sin and things in this world pull us away from You. Please help us, as Your faithful children, to share Your Word with others so they can learn of You. In Your name we pray. Amen.

Jesus Tells about a Sower

Matthew 13:1–23

Take-Home Point
Jesus cares, now and forever!

Today You Need

Leader and Student Materials (p. 10)

Every Lesson Supplies (p. 11)

Learning Area Supplies: pie tin or small cake pan; various large seeds; muffin pan or egg cartons; 2–4 small tongs; a large blanket

Storytelling Supplies: 4 square cake pans; rocks; mud; weeds; soil; medium-size seeds; a small bag; a dried-up plant; a healthy stalk of grain; pictures of plants (optional); 5 pieces of paper

See the Master Supply List on *Leader CD* for complete list for all lessons.

Welcome, *Poster Fun*, and Learning Areas

 **20 minutes**

Play music from the *Leader CD* in the background. Have Helpers with nametags stationed inside and outside of the entrance to greet and direct families to the welcome table. While helping children with nametags and attendance stickers, ask the parents/caregivers to use the *Sign In & Out Sheet* each day. Have the children put their sheep in the sheep pen to take attendance.

SAY: Hi, I'm (Leader's name). (Child's name), **welcome to** *Barnyard Roundup*! **We'll do so many fun activities here. We'll learn more about Jesus and His love for us. We'll hear how He is with us, providing for us and protecting us. You can go to the** *Poster Fun* **table. The Helpers will give you the posters and directions.**

Poster Fun Helpers give out posters and directions. Make sure first and last names are printed on the posters. Remind parents to leave the posters on the table before moving to the next activity. Helpers gather and sort posters alphabetically by last name to prepare for Lesson 4.

Poster Fun for Parents and Kids

You need: your child's *Poster Fun*, yellow crayon, and *Healthy Plant Sticker*

Parents: Make sure you have the same Poster Fun your child used last session. Look at the picture on the front with your child. **SAY: This picture reminds me of the fun you had at** *Barnyard Roundup* **last time. On a farm, farmers grow things. Do you see some plants?** See if your child can point to the sunflowers.

Turn the poster over to the back. Have your child repeat the Lesson 3 Bible Memory Verse after you. Point to the Lesson 3 shepherd staff icon. **SAY: Shepherds can use this tool as a walking stick. God's Word guides us on the right path so we follow God's ways. Color the staff yellow, like a light showing the way.**

Open *Poster Fun* and point to the Lesson 3 picture. **SAY: I see a path with some tiny plants next to it. Do the plants look healthy? No, plants need good soil to grow.** Give your child the *Healthy Plant Sticker*. **SAY: Here is a healthy plant. Do you see some nice, rich soil for it? Stick the** *Healthy Plant Sticker* **in the good soil. When we listen to God's Word, our faith grows healthy and strong. Repeat after me: JESUS LEADS, NOW AND FOREVER.**

Leave the leaflet on the table. Take your child to Learning Area 1. Once your child is engaged in the activity, you may quietly leave.

Transition Activities

Learning Area 1: Make It
Seed Sorting

Goal: Children will exercise their small muscles by picking up seeds and sorting them into an egg carton or muffin pan. **Note:** Closely supervise this activity to ensure that children don't put seeds in their mouth, nose, or ear.

You need: pie tin or small cake pan; various large seeds (e.g., sunflower seeds, corn, beans, pumpkin, or squash); a muffin pan or clean, empty egg cartons; 2–4 small plastic or wooden salad or appetizer tongs

Mix the seeds together in the pie tin. Set the tongs and muffin pan (or egg carton) nearby.

SAY: In our Bible story today, we are going to hear about a farmer who was planting seeds, and we'll learn about how God plants the seed of His Word. Let's look at these seeds. Are they all the same? (No) God made different kinds of seeds for different kinds of plants. We are going to sort the seeds so the same ones are all together. Use your fingers or use these tongs to pick up the seeds and separate them into their own types in the muffin pan sections.

Assist the children as necessary. Tell them the names of the seeds and help them describe how they are different and the same.

Learning Area Options:

Bible Story Coloring Pages (*Leader CD*): Use the lesson's Coloring Page. Helpers can encourage the children to identify objects and people on the Coloring Page. Then they can tell the children that they will be hearing this Bible story a little later.

Another option is to show the children how to draw a simple wheat stalk with a long vertical line and short lines coming off the top of the long line (florets). Allow children to glue some seeds onto the top of the wheat stalk. **SAY:** When a healthy plant grows, it gets a lot of seeds on it. Then those seeds will become other plants! We listen to God's Word and share God's Word with others. We spread His love!

Learning Area 2: Imagine It
Bird Swoop

Goal: The children will learn that seeds must be under the soil to be safe from birds.

You need: nothing

SAY: In today's Bible story, Jesus told a story about a farmer who planted some seeds. Some of the seeds fell on a hard path, and birds came and ate them. Some of you are going to pretend to be seeds, and some of you are going to be birds.

Choose one or two children to be birds; the others will be seeds. Designate one area that will be the path and another that will be the field. **SAY:** Now I am pretending to be the farmer. I am throwing my seeds on the ground, and some of them are going on the hard path. Seeds, when I touch you, you will go to the path and crouch down like a seed. Demonstrate crouching down and making yourself as small as possible. Tap the children on their shoulder one at a time and direct them to go to the path area and crouch down. **Now, we have some hungry birds. They love to eat seeds. They saw the farmer toss some of his seeds on the path. Birds, I want you to swoop down and pretend to eat the seeds.** Demonstrate that the birds should put their arms out and pretend to fly to the path. Then the birds will reach down and put their arms around the seed and pretend to "eat" it. Continue until all seeds have been "eaten."

Learning Area 3: Act It Out
Growing Seeds

Goal: The children will learn what seeds need to grow.

You need: nothing; if you have access to a digital device with a screen large enough for several children to view at one time, you might consider showing a video of the Hap Palmer song "Growing," found online.

SAY: Every plant started out as a seed. We are going to pretend to be seeds and grow. We will find out what seeds need so they can turn into plants. Have a Helper model an action before having the children try.

SAY: First, how can you make your body look like a seed? Encourage the children to crouch on the ground and curl their body down over their feet. **Now I am going to pretend to be the farmer and cover you with nice, rich soil. Now sit down on the floor and stick out your legs, but keep your heads bent over. Your legs are your roots that stick down into the soil to keep your plant body from falling over.**

SAY: I think the seeds need some water. Sometimes God sends rain from the sky. Sometimes a farmer uses sprinklers to water the seeds. I am going to pretend to sprinkle you with water. Walk around the seeds, wiggling your fingers to pretend to sprinkle water over them. **Use your roots to suck up that water.** Demonstrate making a sucking noise. **Slurp, slurp, slurp.**

SAY: Now that you've had some nice water, you need some sunshine. Put your arms up over your head in a circle shape. **I will be the sun and shine on the plants. Oh! I see a tiny shoot sticking out of a plant. Stick one of your arms up to get some sunshine. Here comes another! Put up your other arm. Now the plant is really growing. Keep those roots—your feet—in the ground and stand up. Reach out your arms and pretend you have leaves. Wave your leaves in the wind. Now you are a healthy plant and you will get more seeds on you that the farmer can use to grow more plants.**

SAY: Jesus told a story about a man who planted many seeds. Jesus said God's Word is like seeds. We will learn more about that!

Opening

🕐 **20 minutes**

You need: altar, Lyrics Sheets, *Leader CD*, Puppet Scripts and props, *Polly the Pig Puppet*, bell, Bible

Ring the bell to get everyone's attention. **SING** (to the tune of "The Farmer in the Dell"):

> It's Bible story time. It's Bible story time.
> We're going to hear how Jesus leads.
> It's Bible story time.

Repeat as needed, encouraging the children to sing along as they move toward the altar area and are seated.

SAY: I am so happy to see you again today at our *Barnyard Roundup*. **Who can tell me something special Jesus did for some people who were hungry?** (Accept a few answers.) **Today, we will hear a story Jesus told to remind people to listen to God's Word. We do that when we read the Bible. In the Bible, we learn about how much God loves us. He sent Jesus to be our Savior!** Hold up the Bible.

Show the children how to fold their hands. **SAY: In the name of the Father and of the Son and of the Holy Spirit. Amen. We say those words to remember that God is with us. Now I am going to light the candle to remind us that Jesus is the Light. The sun shines every day, and Jesus shines on us every day!** Light the candle.

SING: "I Am Jesus' Little Lamb" (*Leader CD* Track 15) or "All Together Come and Gather" (*Leader CD* Track 2).

Teach the Take-Home Point

SAY: We already learned that Jesus is our Good Shepherd. He leads His sheep. Where does He lead them? (To places that are good for them) **Where will Jesus take us to be forever?** (Someday, He will lead

us to a wonderful place called heaven! Then we will be with Jesus and others we love forever and ever.) **Today, we will learn about how people hear this Good News. We want this message to be spread all over so everyone knows about our Savior, Jesus.**

SAY: Do you remember how we have a special way at *Barnyard Roundup* **of reminding one another how God has gathered us together to be His children?**

SAY: **GATHER 'ROUND!** (Point up and circle hand.) **JESUS LEADS! KIDS AND LEADERS:** (Point up.) **JESUS LEADS,** (Circle hand.) **NOW AND FOREVER!** Now **let's do it again in a whisper voice.** Repeat Take-Home Point. **Now let's do it in our loudest voice.** Repeat Take-Home Point.

Pray

Have the children sit down. **SAY: Now let's talk to God by praying.** Invite the children to fold their hands, bow their heads, and repeat each phrase of the prayer after you. **SAY: Dear Jesus, / lead us in the ways we should go. / Help us to listen to Your Word / and learn about You / and grow in our faith. / We trust in You, Jesus. / Amen.**

Opening Puppet Skit

You need: *Polly the Pig Puppet*, Puppet Script (*Leader CD*)

Polly is not listening to the farmer's warnings about a hole in the fence.

After the skit, **SAY: Oh, I wonder what Polly will do? I hope she will listen to the farmer.** Let the children share what they think will happen. **Listening is so important, especially listening to God's Word. Let's listen to our Bible story now and find out what Jesus had to say about hearing and following God's Word.**

Bible Storytelling

Pan & seeds and sing!

🕐 **20 minutes**

You need: 4, 8 x 8-inch aluminum cake pans (another size will work, but they must be square or rectangular), each filled with a different item (rocks and/or pebbles, hardened mud that was dried in the sun or baked in an oven, weeds or a real or artificial vinelike plant, and good soil); medium-size seeds (e.g., watermelon seeds); a small bag for the seeds; a shriveled, dried-up plant; a healthy stalk of grain or picture of one printed from the Internet

Gather the children in a circle. Put the four pans in the center of the circle, touching one another. **SAY: One day, Jesus was beside a lake. So many people wanted to hear what He had to say that He talked to them from a boat. He told them a story about a farmer:**

SAY: Once a farmer went out to plant some seeds. Show the seeds in your hand. **He didn't plant the seeds one by one, but he tossed them as he walked along. He tossed lots of seeds all over the place!** Walk around the pans, tossing the seeds so some go in each pan. **Let's look at the different places the seed fell.** Hold up the pan of hardened mud. **Some of the seeds fell on the hard path, and the birds came and ate them.**

SING (to the tune "*The Farmer in the Dell*"):

> **Some seeds fell on the path.**
> **Some seeds fell on the path.**
> **Birds came and ate them up.**
> **Some seeds fell on the path.**

SAY: Will those seeds grow? (No) **Jesus said this is what happens when people hear God's Word and don't understand it. Satan can make them forget what they heard. That's sad.**

Hold up the pan of rocks. **Some of the seeds fell on rocky ground.**

SING (to the tune "*The Farmer in the Dell*"):

> **Some seeds fell on the rocks.**
> **Some seeds fell on the rocks.**
> **(The) sun came and burned them up.**
> **Some seeds fell on the rocks.**

SAY: The seeds that fell in the rocks started to grow, but they did not have much soil for their roots to get water, so when the sun came out, it burned them and they died. Jesus said this is what happens when people joyfully hear God's Word but stop listening when troubles come because they are following Jesus. Show the shriveled plant. **Is this plant healthy? Will this plant get any seeds on it?** (No, it is dead.) **That's sad.**

Show the weedy pan. **Some of the seeds fell among thorns.**

SING (to the tune "*The Farmer in the Dell*"):

> **Some seeds fell in the thorns.**
> **Some seeds fell in the thorns.**
> **Thorns grew and choked the plants.**
> **Some seeds fell in the thorns.**

SAY: The seeds started to grow, but the thorny plants grew up around them and choked them. Jesus said this shows what happens when people hear God's Word but then let other things like money or worries become more important to them than following Jesus.

Sigh. **That's sad. The birds ate some seeds, others were burned up, and some choked. I wonder what will happen in the last pan?** Hold it up.

SING (to the tune "*The Farmer in the Dell*"):

> **Some seeds fell in good soil.**
> **Some seeds fell in good soil.**
> **They grew and made more seeds.**
> **Some seeds fell in good soil.**

Show the grain stalk or the photo of a grain stalk. **SAY: This is what will happen! The plants will grow! Does this plant look healthy or unhealthy (strong or weak)?** (Healthy and strong!) **Jesus said that's what happens with people who hear God's Word and listen to it. They hear the Good News that Jesus is their Savior, and they "bear fruit." Their faith grows, and they share God's Word and serve others in love. We are like the good soil.** Point to the good soil. **We listen to Jesus and follow Him! Jesus leads us and keeps us safe.**

SAY: And look . . . the plants in the good soil will make even more seeds! Point to the seeds on the plant. **Then the farmer can plant more seeds and get *more* plants! As the Holy Spirit makes our faith strong and helps us follow Jesus, people will see God's "fruit" in our lives. That "fruit" isn't seeds, apples, or peaches, but the things we do. We will tell other people about God and His love. And we will do kind and loving things.**

SAY: Let's say our Take-Home Point before going to our next activities: SAY: GATHER 'ROUND! (Point up and circle hand.) **JESUS LEADS! KIDS AND LEADERS:** (Point up.) **JESUS LEADS,** (Circle hand.) **NOW AND FOREVER!**

Ring the bell and **SAY: It's time to move. Follow your Leaders.**

Rotation Sites

🕐 **1 hour**

Early Childhood Teams get into three Rotation Groups. Each Rotation Group moves to their assigned Rotation Site. When it is time to move to a different Rotation Site, ring a bell three times.

Rotation 1: Bible Story Application

🕐 **About 20 minutes**

Review

You need: *Lesson 3 Little Sprouts Early Childhood Leaflet* and stickers, crayons (including multiple crayons of the same color)

Give *Lesson 3 Little Sprouts Early Childhood Leaflets* to the small-group Leaders. Sit at tables or on carpet squares in a circle on the floor. Make sure each child's name gets on his or her leaflet. As you pass out each one, **SAY: This is for Jesus' little lamb** (name of child). **Who knows your name?** (Jesus, the Good Shepherd, knows your name.) **He loves you so much that He shares His precious seed, God's Word, with you. You listen to God's Word and follow Jesus.**

SAY: Look at the picture. Can you point to the hard path? What will happen to the seeds that fell on the hard path? (The birds will eat them.) **Oh yes, I see the birds getting those seeds! Can you point to the rocky soil? Will those seeds grow into healthy plants?** (No) **Why not?** (They don't have deep roots and the hot sun makes them shrivel up.) **Now point to the thorny weeds. Can you see any plants growing?** (No) **Why not?** (The weeds are choking them.) **Now who can tell me where a healthy plant will grow?** (Yes! In the good, rich soil.) **What will be on that plant?** (Yes, more seeds!) **Now let's look inside the leaflet.**

Leaflet Activity

Pass out the stickers for Lesson 3.

SAY: Here is a seed in some soil. We are going to imagine that this seed is in good soil. What color should the good soil be? (Yes, good soil can be brown, yellow, or red.) **Color the soil. Do you see the seed? Point to the seed. Seeds can be different colors, but we will color this seed black.** Children color the seed.

SAY: We are going to think about what the seed needs. What does the seed need to drink? (Water) **Do you see a sticker with drops of water on it? Put it by the seed.** Children add the *Water Sticker* near the soil. **Now what does the seed need to drink the**

water? (Roots) **Point to the roots coming out of the seed into the ground. SAY: Do some of you know of a time when you got sprinkled with water in church?** (Baptism) **When we are baptized with water and God's Word, the Holy Spirit gives us faith. Faith helps you grow strong and healthy.**

SAY: Okay, the seed has water and soil—what else does it need? (Sunshine) **Color the sun in the sky. God tells us His Word is like a light to help us follow Him. Put the *Bible Sticker* near your sun.** The children add the *Bible Sticker*.

The seed grows up toward the sun. Let's draw a plant coming out of the seed, up toward the sun. What color should the plant be? (Green is a good color for a healthy plant.) Assist the children in drawing a line up from the seed. **Jesus said that when we hear God's Word, we grow and bear fruit. Where is a place we hear God's Word?** (Church) **Find the *Church Sticker* and put it next to the plant.** (Children add *Church Sticker*.)

SAY: Now that this healthy plant is growing, what will it get on top? (Blossoms and seeds!) **Let's draw a flower and some seeds on top of the plant.** Assist children as necessary. **Jesus said that as we listen to His Word, He will make a big harvest. Jesus wants all people to know that He's their Savior. He wants all people to live with Him forever in heaven.**

Plants bloom and produce seeds. People produce good works as they share God's love while helping and caring for others. Let's put the *Heart Sticker* in the middle of our seeds. Children add the *Heart Sticker*. **Jesus leads you and gives you ways to follow Him.**

SAY: GATHER 'ROUND! (Point up and circle hand.) **JESUS LEADS! KIDS AND LEADERS:** (Point up.) **JESUS LEADS,** (Circle hand.) **NOW AND FOREVER!**

Or **SING:** "Love in a Box" (*Leader CD* Track 16), reminding the children how we can show God's love to others and spread the seed of God's Word all over!

Rotation 2: Bible Challenge

🕐 **About 20 minutes**

The Bible Memory Song

You need: Bible with the Bible Memory Verse marked, *Bible Memory Songs Sign Chart*, *Leader CD*, and CD player

SAY: Our Bible Memory Verse is "He leads me in paths of righteousness," Psalm 23:3. Those words are from God's book, the Bible. Let's sing this Bible Memory Verse together. **Play** *Leader CD* Track 11. Add the motions as shown on the *Bible Memory Songs Sign Chart*, from the *Leader CD*.

Story Review

You need: nothing (If there are no plants in your area or if you are unable to take the children outside, show some of your own photos, print off pictures of various plants from the Internet, or use the pictures to create a digital slide show to display on a screen that all the children can see.)

Take the students outside. Go for a walk, looking at plants. Make observations about the soil, whether it is soft or hard like the path in the Bible story. Is the soil dry or moist? Look for any birds that might come and snatch away a seed if it was on the ground. Look for any plants growing in rocks or asphalt. Look for weeds that might be choking plants. Find healthy, blooming plants.

Review Song

You need: 5 large pieces of paper, each with one of the following words printed on it in large letters: *Bible, plant, faith, fruit, Jesus*

Sing the following song to the tune of "Bingo." Encourage the children to sing or clap along as they are able. The first sentence reminds the children about the parable. The second sentence explains what the parable means. Then the children help spell out the special word in each stanza as you point to each letter, one at a time. Then the final phrase summarizes the stanza.

1. **There was a farmer sowed some seeds.**
   And God's Word was the name. Yeah!
   (*Do a fist pump into the air on "Yeah!"*)
   B-I-B-L-E, B-I-B-L-E, B-I-B-L-E,
   And God's Word was the name. Yeah! (*Fist pump.*)

2. **There was a farmer sowed some seeds.**
   The Spirit plants the Word deep.
   P-L-A-N-T, P-L-A-N-T, P-L-A-N-T;
   The Spirit works through God's Word.

3. **There was a farmer sowed some seeds,**
   the Word that gives us strong faith:
   F-A-I-T-H, F-A-I-T-H, F-A-I-T-H;
   We're growing strong through God's Word.

4. **There was a farmer sowed some seeds.**
   And God will give a harvest:
   F-R-U-I-T, F-R-U-I-T, F-R-U-I-T;
   The harvest will be fruitful.

5. **There was a farmer sowed some seeds.**
   We tell about the Savior:
   J-E-S-U-S, J-E-S-U-S, J-E-S-U-S;
   We share our Savior, Jesus.

SAY: We want everyone to know about Jesus, our Savior and our Good Shepherd, who leads us, now and forever! We want everyone to know Jesus leads us to heaven.

Rotation 3: Crafts

🕐 20 minutes

Now & Forever Cross

You Need

- *Now & Forever Cross*, 1 per person
- Fine-point permanent markers
- Embellishments, such as glitter glue, *Pony Beads* (sold separately), and *Tipped Yarn Laces* (sold separately)
- Tape
- Chenille wire (optional)
- Cotton swabs and several paper plates (optional)
- Finished sample craft

Make It!

Gather needed materials. Leaders put children's names on the back of their craft.

In advance, if using the cross as a necklace, Leaders attach a yarn lace to the cross for each child before it is decorated. Use tipped yarn laces for easier threading. First, thread a yarn lace through the hole on one arm of the cross. Feed the ends back through the loop and pull snugly. Thread *both* lace ends through one bead to secure in place.

Show the children the supplies.

To make a necklace: Leaders attach the yarn in advance. Before decorating the cross, the children can thread beads on the separate pieces of yarn in a pattern of their choosing. Help and encourage the children as needed. You may need to tape down the yarn and cross to the table to prevent it from moving as the children work.

When children have added all the beads they want to one side, Leaders tie a knot in the yarn to hold the beads in place. Children repeat the procedure to thread beads on the second piece of yarn.

When children have completed threading beads, Leaders tie the ends of the yarn to make a necklace.

Color the cross with permanent markers and decorate with glitter glue, if desired.

To make an ornament: Children create a hanger by bending and attaching a chenille wire, or Leaders attach five inches of yarn.

To decorate: Children color the cross with permanent markers. You may want to encourage them to work on coloring only the letters, or on coloring everything that is *not* a letter (the cross outline and background lines). Show the finished sample craft(s). Be sure to touch

each letter and say its name, and then read the words inside the cross.

If desired, provide glitter glue for the children to use on the cross outline. If children can't squeeze the glitter glue container, squeeze a pile of the glue onto a paper plate, and let the children use the tips of cotton swabs to dab the glue onto the cross. Allow to dry.

Putting It All Together

SAY: Shepherds lead their sheep along safe paths to keep them from harm. Our Good Shepherd, Jesus, leads us in the paths of righteousness, the way that leads to God. In fact, Jesus is the way to God. He gives us forgiveness for our sins and eternal life.

But how do people learn that Jesus is their Good Shepherd? Through God's Word! And how does Jesus lead His sheep? Through God's Word! The Holy Spirit works through God's Word to produce faith in Jesus and to help faith grow.

Today, you will make a *Now & Forever Cross* to remind you that Jesus leads you, now and forever.

SAY: GATHER 'ROUND! (Point up and circle hand.) JESUS LEADS! **KIDS AND LEADERS:** (Point up.) JESUS LEADS, (Circle hand.) NOW AND FOREVER!

Or make a *Now & Forever Heart* using your cross.

You'll need red construction paper cut into large hearts; glue; markers; and embellishments, such as stickers, seeds, or glitter markers. To make the hearts, Leaders cut out the hearts and glue the *Now & Forever Cross* onto the middle. Across the top of the heart, Leaders write "Jesus leads." Children decorate the heart using the supplies as desired.

Snack

🕐 **20 minutes**

Scattering Seeds

You Need

- A bowl and plastic fork for each child
- A bowl of cooked wagon wheel pasta
- A bowl of thawed frozen corn
- Separate bowls of assorted mix-ins, such as black beans, diced tomatoes, shredded cheese, chopped cilantro, diced avocado
- A bowl of premixed dressing for the pasta salad
- A large bowl and a large serving spoon
- Hand sanitizer & napkins
- Cups & water

Advance Preparation

Cook and drain the pasta. Add olive oil. Prepare desired mix-ins. Prepare salad dressing. For each session, provide enough ingredients for the Team to make a batch of pasta salad. Before groups arrive, put all items listed above on *each* Team's table.

> **Suggested Dressing Recipe** (for 1 lb. pasta):
> 1½ c. salsa, ⅓ c. olive oil, 3 Tbsp. lime juice, 3–4 cloves minced garlic, salt, pepper

When Kids Arrive

Take the children to the restroom. Have them wash their hands. Have them sit in their places. **SAY: Welcome to Bountiful Blessings! SAY: GATHER 'ROUND!** (Point up and circle hand.) **JESUS LEADS! KIDS AND LEADERS:** (Point up.) **JESUS LEADS,** (Circle hand.) **NOW AND FOREVER! SAY: Today's Bible story is a parable about a farmer who plants seeds by walking through the field, scattering seeds by hand. Nowadays, farmers use machines to do their work! Farmers today often use a machine called a seeder to plant corn in fields.**

SAY: God's Word is like seed corn. God spreads His Word of life and salvation for all to everyone. He gathers us to Himself! Let's say the Bible verse: "He leads me in paths of righteousness." Psalm 23:3.

Making the Snack

SAY: Our snack will help you remember that God plants faith in our hearts like farmers plant seed. Today, your Team will work together to make pasta salad. Let each person add an ingredient to the salad. Hold up each ingredient as you explain: **The first ingredient is pasta. This pasta looks like wheels to remind us of the tractors and seeders that farmers use to plant seeds. The next ingredient is corn. This reminds us of the seeds farmers plant. And Jesus said God's Word is like the seed. Jesus leads us through God's Word.** Add the other ingredients. Name and show each of the other salad mix-ins the kids can add.

SAY: Last, pour the dressing over the salad. Gently mix it all together. Make sure everyone gets a turn to stir. Hold up the finished example. Lead a snack prayer. Thank Jesus for the food and for leading us as our faith in Him grows. Leaders serve the pasta salad or assist the children as needed in passing the bowl around the table to share the "seeds" with everyone.

Before They Go

SAY: A farmer plants and cares for seeds so they produce a bountiful harvest. Through the seed of God's Word, Jesus is leading us. He helps our faith to grow and bear fruit.

Games

🕐 **20 minutes**

Count the Corn

You Need

- 4 potato sacks (or pillow cases)
- Lots of dry corn on the cob, carrots, or other vegetables that can be collected (or plastic play food)
- 4 baskets
- Stopwatch

Get Ready

Set food in a long line on one side of playing area (think trough, not piles). Line up the four baskets on the other side of the playing area, with plenty of space between each one.

Here We Go

SAY: Folks, welcome back to Bales of Fun Games! Jesus told a story about a farmer who plants seed and wants it to grow. *What sorts of things do plants need to grow?* (Sun, rain, good soil, no bugs) **All those things help plants grow lots of wheat or vegetables! Farmers care for their seeds as they grow. Jesus cares for us and gives us His Word to make us healthy and strong, and to lead us in the paths He wants us to go.**

SAY: GATHER 'ROUND! (Point up and circle hand.) JESUS LEADS! **KIDS AND LEADERS:** (Point up.) JESUS LEADS, (Circle hand.) NOW AND FOREVER!

Divide the children into four Teams and have each Team line up behind a basket (and potato sack). Demonstrate the relay as you explain each step.

SAY: When I say "Go!" the first person in line will run across to the other side. Once there, pick up one piece of food, place it under your chin, and carefully run back to the basket without touching your food with your hands. Stop and put your food in the basket; then go to the end of the line and sit down. It will be the next person in line's turn to go. We're going to see how much food your Team can harvest in five minutes. Do you think we can fill our baskets?

Use the stopwatch, but be sure to let everyone have a turn. Once your group has done the relay by running down to harvest the food, make it more challenging by having them use the potato sacks. Show them how to put their feet inside a sack, hold onto the edge, jump down to the food, put the food under their chin,

and jump back. To make the relay easier, shorten the distance between the basket and the food.

After everyone had a turn with the potato sacks, **SAY: Good job gathering all the corn** (vegetables)**! Farmers want a big harvest, so when farmers plant seeds, do they just throw it anywhere?** (No) **Right, they want to make sure that every seed is in the best place possible to grow. Jesus told the Bible story to show that He wants all people to hear God's Word. How can you help spread the seed of the Good News of Jesus Christ?** (Tell others about Jesus, bring a friend to Sunday School, help your neighbor) **By His example, Jesus leads us to share His saving grace with others.**

Fun in the Play Yard

If your Games time is in a play yard, consider using activities from the Learning Area too. Bird Swoop is a possibility. You will need a larger comforter or blanket. Add one more dimension to the game. After the kids have been "eaten," act out what happens if the seeds fall upon good soil. **SAY: When the farmer was tossing his seeds, some of them fell on good soil. Soil is another name for dirt. The seeds sank into the soil where the birds could not see them. This time, when I toss the seeds, I want you to crouch down in the field area.** Tap the children on their shoulder one by one and have them crouch. **Now, I am going to cover you with this blanket, which is like the soil that covers the seeds. Birds, you are still very hungry, so it is time to fly around the field.** Birds do so. **Do you see any seeds? No? Oh, too bad, no seeds for you today! The seeds are safe. They can grow!**

Note: Another option is to put the blanket over the top of a table to hide seeds that are crouched underneath it.

Closing

🕐 **about 20 minutes**

Closing Puppet Skit

You need: *Polly the Pig Puppet*, Puppet Script, *Lesson 3 Little Sprouts Early Childhood Leaflet*, *Lesson 3 My Shepherd Collectible*, children's take-home items

Seat the children on the floor or carpet squares. **SING:** "My Shepherd" (*Leader CD* Track 17). Bring out *Polly the Pig Puppet* to talk about what happens when we don't follow our leaders and when we don't listen to God's Word. Use the Puppet Script from the *Leader CD*.

After the skit, close with this echo prayer: **Dear Jesus, / thank You for being with us / at *Barnyard Roundup* today. / Help us to remember / that You lead us now /and forever. / Help us trust You always. / In Your name we pray. Amen.**

SAY: Let's meet again at *Barnyard Roundup*! Next time, we'll hear how Jesus always loves us, no matter what. It's great to know He forgives our sins. **SAY: GATHER 'ROUND!** (Point up and circle hand.) **JESUS LEADS! KIDS AND LEADERS:** (Point up.) **JESUS LEADS,** (Circle hand.) **NOW AND FOREVER! Now let's do it again in a whisper voice.** (Repeat Take-Home Point.) **Now let's do it in our loudest voice.** (Repeat Take-Home Point.)

Show a lesson leaflet. **SAY: Please take this home and ask your Mom or Dad to read it. There is something special on the front and back page for your family to do together.**

Thank your Helpers. Send home *Lesson 3 Little Sprouts Early Childhood Leaflet*, *Lesson 3 My Shepherd Collectible*, and other take-home items. As you say good-bye to children at sign-out time, remind parents to read the leaflet at home.

Looking Ahead

Pray for your students and Helpers.

Restock or prepare Learning Area with Lesson 4 materials. Use the grass from Lesson 2.

Lay out *Poster Fun* from *Little Sprouts Early Childhood Leaflets* for the next lesson's transition activity.

Prepare the Storytelling materials.

Review the next lesson's plans. Ask your team members what adjustments might improve the schedule or activities.

Lesson 4

Roundup Leader Devotion

Bible Story: Jesus Tells about a Lost Son
Luke 15:11–32

Bible Memory Verse:
"I will fear no evil, for You are with me." Psalm 23:4

Read Luke 15:11–32 and
Think on These Things:

This parable of the Lost Son is in the middle of a series of parables about "lost" things—a lost sheep, a lost coin, and now, a lost son.

Luke 15:11–16 The father's property and livestock make us think of a farm homestead, but we know from the Bible text that this family also lived in a populated area. The son rudely confronted the father, demanding the inheritance that would be his at his father's death. When his father gives him his share, the son foolishly leaves his family and wastes his inheritance. A famine hits, and he ends up hungry and alone at a farm, far from home, feeding pods to pigs that belonged to Gentiles. What a desperate, pathetic position for a young Jewish man!

Luke 15:17–24 The son has plenty of time to regret his circumstances. He decides to return to his father, confess his sin and his unworthiness, and beg to be one of his father's servants. Meanwhile, back at the farm, the father has been waiting and watching for his son. While the son is still a long way off, his father sees him and feels compassion. The father abandons his dignity to run to his son and welcome him home. The father calls to his servants to cover his son's shame with a fine robe and his wayward feet with shoes. He throws a party to celebrate his son's return.

Luke 15:25–32 When the older brother finds out about the celebration for the return of his brother, he's angry. The gracious, loving father goes out to him and asks him also to join the celebration that his brother, who was lost and as good as dead, is now home—found and alive.

This is a Gospel story about a forgiving father. God our Father rejoices when the lost is found. Our good, gracious, and merciful God even rejoices over people like you and me who have acted as if He were dead, wasted all His rich gifts, and then tried to deal with Him as if His love were something we can earn. Instead, our loving Father covers our sin and shame with the blood of Jesus. He nourishes us in the celebration of the Lord's Supper, where we are forgiven, restored, and saved for all eternity. Once dead in our sin, we are now alive; we who were lost are found in Jesus Christ.

Take-Home Point:
Jesus forgives, now and forever!

Just like you and me, kids get in trouble! We are all sinners. We do what we want instead of what God wants. Just like the son in the Bible story, we don't assume that, should we turn from sin, we will find forgiveness. Instead, we expect the judgment and punishment we deserve.

Jesus Gathers Us Together: God our Father sent His beloved and only Son, Jesus, to save us. By His life, death, and resurrection, Jesus paid for our sins, redeemed us, and earned for us eternal life. We "fear no evil" because Jesus, our Good Shepherd, is with us, now and forever. Jesus finds us, forgives us, gathers us together in His family, and gives us abundant life, now and forever.

Prayer: Dear Jesus, thank You for Your unconditional love. Forgive us when we sin and get mixed up with the things of this world. Thank You for gathering us into Your loving flock even when we wander far away. You protect us from sin and evil. Help us to walk with You. We love You, Jesus. Thank You for loving us. In Your name we pray. Amen.

Jesus Tells about the Lost Son

Luke 15:11–32

Today You Need

Leader and Student Materials (p. 10)

Every Lesson Supplies (p. 11)

Learning Area Supplies: a toy barn; toy farm animals; a plastic tub with green shredded paper (from Lesson 2); a large basket; beanbags; robe (optional)

Storytelling Supplies: white board, marker, bag of coins

See the Master Supply List on *Leader CD* for complete list for all lessons.

Welcome, *Poster Fun*, and Learning Areas

🕐 **20 minutes**

Play music from the *Leader CD* in the background. Have Helpers with nametags stationed inside and outside of the entrance to greet and direct families to the welcome table. While helping children with nametags and attendance stickers, ask the parents/caregivers to use the *Sign In & Out Sheet* each day. Have the children put their sheep in the sheep pen to take attendance.

SAY: Hi, I'm (Leader's name). (Child's name), **welcome to** *Barnyard Roundup*! **We'll do so many fun activities here. We'll learn more about Jesus and His love for us. We'll hear how He is with us, providing for us and protecting us. You can go to the** *Poster Fun* **table. The Helpers will give you the posters and directions.**

Poster Fun Helpers give out posters and directions. Make sure first and last names are printed on the posters. Remind parents to leave the posters on the table before moving to the next activity. Helpers gather and sort posters alphabetically by last name to prepare for Lesson 5.

Poster Fun for Parents and Kids

You need: your child's *Poster Fun*, red crayon, and *Lost Son Sticker*

Parents: Make sure you have the same *Poster Fun* your child used last time. Look at the picture on the front with your child. **SAY: This picture reminds me of the fun you had at** *Barnyard Roundup* **last time. Can you show me the barn? Which animals stay in a barn? The barn is where the animals can stay warm and safe.**

Turn the poster over to the back page. Have your child repeat the Lesson 4 Bible Memory Verse after you. Point to the Lesson 4 shepherd staff icon. **SAY: Shepherds use this special tool to rescue sheep who are lost or hurt. The curved handle can pull a sheep out of trouble. Color the staff red.**

Open *Poster Fun* and point to the Lesson 4 picture. **SAY: How do you think this man feels?** (Happy)

Give your child the *Lost Son Sticker*. **SAY: What can you tell about this man?** (He's had a hard time.) **Today, you will learn that the happy man is the father of this poor man. The son left home, and when he came back, his father was so happy to see him! He ran to give his son a hug.** Assist your child in adding the *Lost Son Sticker* in the father's arms. **Repeat after me: JESUS FORGIVES, NOW AND FOREVER.**

Leave the leaflet on the table. Take your child to Learning Area 1. Once your child is engaged in the activity, you may quietly leave.

Transition Activities

Learning Area 1: Make It
Finding Lost Treasures

Goal: The children will search for animals in the grass and put them in a barn.

You need: a toy barn (or one made out of a box), toy farm animals, a shallow plastic tub (such as an under-bed storage container) with the green shredded paper from Lesson 2 (or green Easter grass)

Set the barn beside the tub of "grass." Hide the animals in the grass.

SAY: In our Bible story today, we are going to hear about someone who was lost and then came back home. Where do farm animals go to stay warm and safe? (A barn) **There are lost animals in this grass. Can you find them and put them in the barn?**

Discuss the names of the farm animals. **SAY: I wonder how the animals got lost? I'm glad you're here to help them find their way back to the barn. Today, we will hear about a son who was lost. But then he came back! He wasn't lost anymore.**

Learning Area Options:

Bible Story Coloring Pages (*Leader CD*): Use the lesson's Coloring Page. Helpers can encourage the children to identify objects and people on the Coloring Page. Then they can tell the children that they will be hearing this Bible story a little later.

Learning Area 2: Imagine It
Pig Food Toss

Goal: The children will practice throwing "food" into a trough for pigs.

You need: a tub or large basket, beanbags (or crumpled up pieces of paper or dry corn cobs, if available)

SAY: In today's Bible story, a man left his father and his home. He lost all his money. The only job he could get was feeding pigs. A trough is a container that holds food for pigs. We are going to pretend this is a pig trough and throw the food into the trough. What do you think pigs eat? (Accept answers. Pig owners buy pig food made from corn or wheat or soybeans, but pigs also eat plants and animals, so they eat many different things, such as grasses, roots, fruits, worms, insects, trees, and even garbage.) **In our Bible story today, the pigs were fed carob pods.**

Put a piece of masking tape on the floor three to four feet away from the tub or basket. Allow the children to take turns standing behind the line and tossing

corn cobs from nursery

the "food" (beanbags, paper, or corn cobs) into the container. Don't keep score. Allow the children to take several turns, and encourage them as they improve.

SAY: Would you like to eat this food? Would you eat pods from a tree or corn cobs or even garbage? (No. The food that pigs eat is not good for us to eat.) **But in our story, the man was so hungry that he wanted to eat the pigs' food! That's when he decided to go back home. Do you think his father will forgive him and give him something to eat? Jesus, our Good Shepherd, always loves and forgives us, even when think we don't need him.**

Learning Area 3: Act It Out
Father, May I?

cute / like Simon Says

Goal: The children will take steps to return to the father.

You need: nothing, robe (or large shirt) to put on the father (optional)

SAY: In our story today, a young man left his father's house. His father gave him some money, but after he spent it all, he decided he wanted to go back home. But he was worried that his father would not forgive him for wasting the money.

Designate one child as the father. Put the father at one end of the room. At the other end, have the children sit down. One child at a time will stand up to have a turn being the son.

SAY: The son wants to go back to the father. So the son will say, "Father, I am sorry. Please forgive me. May I run back home?" Or you can pick another way to move instead of running. You can say, "May I skip back home?" or "May I tiptoe back home?" Or any other way you choose.

The father will say, "I forgive you. Yes, you may." Then the son will run (or skip or whatever movement he chose) **to get to the father. They will hug each other because they are so happy to be back together!** Note: If your children are uncomfortable hugging, another kind gesture can be used, such as a high five.

After a few turns, choose a different father. You may want to practice the sayings and responses a few times, or shorten them, especially if you have very young children.

SAY: When we do things that are wrong, we are sorry. We can tell Jesus we are sorry, and He will always forgive us. Jesus died on the cross to take our sins away and will love and forgive us, now and always.

Opening

⏲ 20 minutes

You need: altar, Lyrics Sheets, *Leader CD*, Puppet Scripts and props, *Polly the Pig Puppet*, bell, Bible

Ring the bell to get everyone's attention. **SING** (to the tune of "The Farmer in the Dell"):

> It's Bible story time. It's Bible story time.
> We're going to hear how God forgives.
> It's Bible story time!

Repeat as needed, encouraging the children to sing along as they move toward the altar area and are seated.

SAY: I am so happy to see you again at our *Barnyard Roundup*. Who can tell me something you learned last time about seeds? Accept a few answers. **Today, we will hear a story Jesus told to remind people that God will always love them and forgive them. This story is in the Bible.** Hold up the Bible.

Show the children how to fold their hands. **SAY: In the name of the Father and of the Son and of the Holy Spirit. Amen. We say those words to remember that God is with us. Now I am going to light the candle to remind us that Jesus is the Light. The sun shines every day, and Jesus shines on us every day!** Light the candle.

SING: "I Am Jesus' Little Lamb" (*Leader CD* Track 15) or "All Together Come and Gather" (*Leader CD* Track 2).

Teach the Take-Home Point

SAY: Show me with your face how you would feel if someone took a toy from you. Show me how you would feel if someone hurt you. Wait for responses. **Yes, I see some sad or even angry faces. Now show me with your face how your mom or dad or grandparents would feel if you didn't listen to them and if you didn't do what you were supposed to.** Wait for responses. **Yes, your parents or grandparents would not be happy. But would they still love you?** (Of course!) **Would they forgive you?** (Yes!) **Because they love you, your parents will forgive you for the wrong that you did. What you did was not okay—it was still a sin—but they will still love you.**

SAY: GATHER 'ROUND! (Point up and circle hand.) **JESUS FORGIVES! KIDS AND LEADERS:** (Point up.) **JESUS FORGIVES,** (Circle hand.) **NOW AND FOREVER!** Now let's do it again in a whisper voice. Repeat Take-Home Point. **Now let's do it in our loudest voice.** Repeat Take-Home Point.

Pray

Have the children sit down. **SAY: Now let's talk to God by praying.** Invite the children to fold their hands, bow their heads, and repeat each phrase of the prayer after you. Pause after each forward slash mark (/).

SAY: Dear Father, / we don't always do what we should. / Help us to be sorry / when we do wrong. / Thank You for always forgiving us / because Jesus died on the cross. / We love You! / Amen.

Opening Puppet Skit

You need: *Polly the Pig Puppet*, Puppet Script (*Leader CD*)

Polly is jealous of all the attention Perry gets when he returns to the farm.

After the skit, **SAY: I'm really glad Perry came back, aren't you? It was so merciful of the farmer to take such great care of him instead of just giving him a lecture about what a bad pig he was for leaving. Perry already had consequences for his choice when he got hurt and scared; he already felt sorry for what he had done. The farmer was very forgiving.**

SAY: We are going to hear a story Jesus told about someone who left home and decided to come back. Listen to find out whether he's sorry and to see how his father and his brother react when he comes home.

Bible Storytelling

🕐 **20 minutes**

You need: white board or large piece of white chart paper taped to a wall or easel, dry erase or regular marker, bag (clear sandwich or drawstring) of real or toy coins

You will be drawing on the white board or paper to tell the story. Use very simple stick drawings and don't worry about being a great artist. You will also be taking money out of the bag, little by little. You may want to let a child (especially one who might need extra help focusing) or several children have a turn doing this.

Gather the children in front of the board/paper. **SAY: Jesus told a story about how God loves and forgives.**

Draw a house. Outside the house, draw three stick figures. The one in the middle should have a robe. As you're drawing, **SAY: There was a man who had two sons. He had a nice house and lots of money. One of the sons decided that he wanted to go away. He asked his father for some money and left.** Erase or cross out one of the men. Shake the bag of coins.

Draw a stick person off by himself. **SAY: When the son left, he began to spend his money. Maybe he stayed at a nice place and spent some of his money.** Draw a rectangle with several windows and pillars in front. Take some of the money out of the bag. **Maybe he went to some parties and spent more money.** Draw some musical notes to represent dancing. Take some more money out of the bag. **Maybe he bought his friends presents and food that cost a lot of money.** Draw a present and a plate with squiggles of food on it. Take more money out of the bag. **Maybe he bought some nice clothes and sandals and spent more money.** Draw a striped robe. Take some more money out. **Since his friends knew he had lots of money, maybe they asked him for some and he gave some to them.** Draw two or three other stick figures near the man. Take the last of the money out of the bag.

SAY: The Bible doesn't say exactly how he spent the money, but we know that soon it was all gone. Show the empty bag. **Now the son didn't have any more money to buy food, clothes, or a place to stay. How do your mom and dad get money?** (Yes, they have a job.) **So the son got a job. His job was to feed the pigs. Draw a pig. Does that sound like a fun job?** (Accept answers.) **The pigs were dirty and smelly. The food he had to feed them was yucky. But the son was so hungry because he had nothing to eat, that he even wanted to eat the pigs' food!**

SAY: Then he thought about his home and his father. Draw a circle around the home and figures that you first drew. **Perhaps he thought, "Maybe if I go back and tell my father I am sorry, he will let me work for him. It won't be the same as being his son, but I know he treats his workers well." So the son decided to go back home.** Flip the chart paper or erase the previous drawings. Draw the house again at the top and a path leading from the house. At the end of the path, draw the son.

SAY: The father had been watching for his son. When he saw that the son was coming back, the father ran to him and hugged him. Draw the father running on the path. Make one leg stick out or use lines behind him to show movement. **The son said, "I have sinned against God and against you. I don't deserve to be called your son." But the father gave him a new robe and a ring and new shoes, and he told his servants to get a big party ready. He said, "My son was lost and now is found!"**

SAY: God is like this Father. Even when we do bad things and don't deserve it, God still loves us and forgives us, and we are still His children. God the Father sent *His* Son, Jesus, to die on the cross and take our sins away. Because of Jesus, God loves and forgives us, no matter what we do. SAY: GATHER 'ROUND! (Point up and circle hand.) **JESUS FORGIVES! KIDS AND LEADERS:** (Point up.) **JESUS FORGIVES,** (Circle hand.) **NOW AND FOREVER!**

Ring the bell and **SAY: It's time to move. Follow your Leaders.**

Rotation Sites

🕐 **1 hour**

Early Childhood Teams get into three Rotation Groups. Each Rotation Group moves to their assigned Rotation Site. When it is time to move to a different Rotation Site, ring a bell three times.

Rotation 1: Bible Story Application

🕐 **20 minutes**

Review

You need: *Lesson 4 Little Sprouts Early Childhood Leaflet* and stickers, crayons

Give *Lesson 4 Little Sprouts Early Childhood Leaflets* to small-group Leaders. Sit at tables or on carpet squares in a circle on the floor. Make sure each child's name gets on his or her leaflet. As you pass out each one, **SAY: This is for Jesus' little lamb** (name of child). When all the leaflets are distributed, **SAY: Point to your name. Who knows your name?** (Jesus, the Good Shepherd, knows your name.) **You are one of His precious children, and He died on the cross to take all your sin away. Because of what Jesus did, you are forgiven!**

Look at the picture. Do you see the father? Point to the father. Children point to the father. **What is he doing?** (Hugging someone) **Whom is he hugging?** (His son who was lost) **Can you point to the son?** Children point to the son. **How does the son look? What do you notice about his clothes?** (His clothes look dirty and torn.) **Why do they look that way?** (He had a job feeding the pigs.) **He just came back home. Is the father happy to see him?** (Yes) **How can you tell that the father is happy?** (The father is smiling.) **Now let's look inside the leaflet.**

Leaflet Activity

Pass out the stickers for *Lesson 4.*

SAY: I see some children at preschool. Point to the picture of the boy with the car. Help the children find the scene on their leaflets. **What do you think is happening?** (The child took the car from his friend.) **Is it nice to take a toy from someone else?** (No) **What could the boy do?** (He could say he is sorry and give the toy back) **This boy did something he shouldn't have done. That is called a sin. Jesus died on the cross to pay for this boy's sin. He is forgiven. Let's put a *Cross Sticker* by the picture of the boy to help us remember that God still loves him and that God**

always loves us too. Children put the *Cross Sticker* next to or on top of the scene.

SAY: Look at the picture in the middle of the page. It looks like this girl is yelling at her teacher! I wonder what happened. (Allow the children to suggest reasons why the girl might be arguing with her teacher, such as not wanting to leave the sensory table or not liking the items found on the sensory table.) **Do you think she should do that?** (No, it is very disrespectful to yell at a teacher or anyone else.) **Is that a sin?** (Yes) **What should the girl do?** (Yes, she should say she is sorry.) **Do you think her teacher will forgive her?** (Yes) **I'm sure the teacher knows that Jesus forgives her, now and forever. Let's put another *Cross Sticker* next to her.** Children put the *Cross Sticker* next to the picture on their leaflets.

SAY: Do you see any other pictures of people doing things they shouldn't do? Oh dear! It looks like a girl is pushing a boy off his chair. Why do you think she is doing that? (She wants a turn doing the art project.) **I hope she says she is sorry and the boy forgives her. Will God forgive her and still love her?** (Yes, He will, because Jesus died on the cross to take her sin away.) **Let's put the last *Cross Sticker* on the page, beside her.** Children put the *Cross Sticker* next to or on top of the picture. Allow children time to finish coloring the picture.

Review the Take-Home Point. **SAY: GATHER 'ROUND!** (Point up and circle hand.) **JESUS FORGIVES! KIDS AND LEADERS:** (Point up.) **JESUS FORGIVES,** (Circle hand.) **NOW AND FOREVER! Now let's do it again in a whisper voice.** (Repeat Take-Home Point.) **Now let's do it in our loudest voice.** (Repeat Take-Home Point.)

SING: "God Is Near" (*Leader CD* Track 14).

Rotation 2: Bible Challenge

🕐 **About 20 minutes**

The Bible Memory Song

You need: Bible with the Bible Memory Verse marked, *Bible Memory Songs Sign Chart, Leader CD,* and CD player

SAY: Our Bible Memory Verse is "I will fear no evil, for You are with me," Psalm 23:4. Those words are from God's book, the Bible. Let's sing this Bible Memory Verse together. Play *Leader CD* Track 12. Add the motions as shown on the *Bible Memory Songs Sign Chart,* from the *Leader CD.*

Story Review

You need: the bag of coins from Bible Storytelling; make sure you have at least 1 coin for each child in your group

Seat the children in a circle. Hold the bag of coins.

SAY: In Jesus' story, the son asked his father for some money and then left home.

SING (to the tune of "Here We Go 'Round the Mulberry Bush," singing "(The)" on the upbeat), clapping and encouraging the children to clap along while you sing:

(The) son said, "Please give / some money to me."
Some money to me. Some money to me.
(The) son said, "Please give / some money to me.
So I can / live on my own now."

SAY: We are going to pretend we are the son and we have this bag of money. We will pass around the bag of money. When the money bag gets to you, take out a coin and say something you think the son may have spent it on. You may need to give the children some suggestions (e.g., food, parties, a place to stay, clothes, shoes, presents, friends). Children are likely to repeat what other children say. That is okay. The goal is to move the money bag around the circle of children until it is empty.

(The) son said, "Oh no! / The money's all gone!
The money's all gone! The money's all gone!
(The) son said, "Oh no! / The money's all gone!
So I must / find a good job now."

Collect coins from the children; return them to the bag.

SAY: Where did the son get a job? (Feeding pigs) **Let's pretend to toss food to the pigs while I sing the next part. The pigs and their food are smelly. Hold your nose while you toss the food.** Demonstrate holding your nose with one hand and pretending to toss food with the other.

SING (holding your nose while you sing, if you'd like):

(The) son said, "Now I / must feed all these pigs.
Feed all these pigs. Feed all these pigs.
(The) son said, "Now I / must feed all these pigs.
I want some / pig food myself, though.

SAY: Finally, the son decided to go home and ask his father to forgive him. But while the son was still a long way away from his home, his father saw him coming and ran to him to hug him! Give yourself a hug as I sing.

SING:

(The) father said, "Son, / I'm so glad you're back.
I'm so glad you're back.
I'm so glad you're back."
(The) father said, "Son, / I'm so glad you're back.
So now let's / go have a party!"

SAY: Jesus is glad when we say we're sorry. He forgives us for the times when we do whatever we want and don't do the things we should. **SAY: GATHER 'ROUND!** (Point up and circle hand.) **JESUS FORGIVES! KIDS AND LEADERS:** (Point up.) **JESUS FORGIVES,** (Circle hand.) **NOW AND FOREVER! Now let's do it again in a whisper voice.** (Repeat Take-Home Point.) **Now let's do it in our loudest voice.** (Repeat Take-Home Point.)

Rotation 3: Crafts

🕐 **20 minutes**

Forgiven Suncatcher

You Need

- Forgiven Suncatcher, 1 per child
- Suncatcher paints and fine paintbrushes
- Paper plate, 1 per color
- Stable cup (e.g., clean, empty egg carton)
- Paint smocks (or over-size shirts), 1 per child
- Tape and newspaper or plastic tablecloth
- Toothpicks
- Eye droppers, 1 per color
- Tipped Yarn Laces (sold separately), narrow fabric ribbon, or curling ribbon
- Fine-point permanent markers
- Finished sample craft

Make It!

Gather supplies. Leaders use a permanent marker to put the child's name on the back of the craft.

In advance, put each color of paint in sturdy individual cups that aren't likely to tip over. Set cups and an eye dropper on paper plates. Cover the work surface (table) and floor with the newspaper and tape down.

Show children the finished sample craft so they can see how the light shines through it. The suncatcher paint becomes more clear when it dries.

Show children the supplies. Emphasize that each eye dropper must stay with its paint so colors don't mix.

Remind children to be very careful with the paint, as it is nonwashable. Help them to put on paint smocks.

Show children how to use the eye droppers to squeeze a small amount of paint onto one section of the suncatcher. Emphasize that if they use too much paint or squeeze too hard, the paint will be too thick and the sun won't be able to shine through. Demonstrate how to use a toothpick to spread the paint around within a section. Use a new toothpick for each color. Provide paintbrushes for larger sections, but toothpicks may give the children better control.

Let the children paint the suncatcher. Help and encourage them as needed. After the suncatchers dry, string ribbon or laces through the top hole for hanging.

Putting It All Together

SAY: In today's story, the son made some bad choices. He finally realized he had sinned, and then he went home to ask his father for forgiveness.

We make bad choices too. We don't always obey our Father in heaven and what He says in His Word. We get into trouble. We sin. But because Jesus died on the cross for us, our heavenly Father welcomes us back. He forgives our sin and gives us a home in heaven.

Gather a Great Idea!

For additional ideas, like *Cock-a-Doodle-Do Jesus Loves You Rooster*, see the Bonus Crafts in the *Craft Leader Guide*. The rooster can remind the children each morning that Jesus forgives them. He always will love them, no matter what, as sure as the sun rises and the rooster crows each morning.

Snack

🕐 20 minutes

All Mixed Up

You Need

- A plastic zipper bag for each child
- Popcorn, mini marshmallows, dried cranberries, sunflower seeds, each in separate bowls
- Serving spoons or scoops
- Optional additional mix-ins: coconut flakes, chopped dried apricots, broken pretzel sticks, chocolate chips, yogurt-covered raisins
- Hand sanitizer, napkins, cups, and water

Advance Preparation

Before each group arrives, put items listed above on each Team's table.

When Kids Arrive

Take the children to the restroom. Have them wash their hands. Have them sit in their places.

SAY: Howdy! Today, you are learning that Jesus forgives. That's such a blessing because we are all sinners. We do what we want, instead of what God wants us to do. We get what is most important in our lives mixed up. Thankfully, Jesus died and rose again. He paid for our sins. Jesus calls us back to Himself and forgives us, no matter how mixed up things get. Today, our snack will remind us of that.

SAY: GATHER 'ROUND! (Point up and circle hand.) JESUS FORGIVES! **TEAMS:** (Point up.) **JESUS FORGIVES,** (Circle hand.) **NOW AND FOREVER!**

SAY: Today's Bible story is a parable about someone who got all mixed up and sinned. When he asked his father for forgiveness, his father forgave him! We get mixed up and sin too. We say unkind things and don't listen to our parents. Today's verse reminds us that Jesus, our Good Shepherd, is always with us and protects us from sin. Let's say today's verse: "I will fear no evil, for You are with me," Psalm 23:4.

Making the Snack

SAY: Our snack today is all mixed up! Hold up your finished example. **Each of the ingredients in this snack mix reminds you of what we learn at** *Barnyard Roundup*. Demonstrate as you explain, and then let the children take turns preparing their own bags:

- You will work with a partner. Open your bag. Have one person hold the bag with both hands, one on each side, keeping the bag open and holding it above the table and bowl. Working together shows love. Jesus FORGIVES. We aren't lost and away from God anymore; He is with us.
- Put in a scoop of marshmallows. Marshmallows are fluffy and white, like sheep. A shepherd cares for sheep. Jesus CARES for us.
- Now, add a scoop of dried cranberries. Dried cranberries are sweet, and it is sweet to trust that Jesus PROVIDES for us.
- Put in two scoops of popcorn. Then add a scoop of sunflower seeds. We learned that farmers sow seeds abundantly, and God's Word is shared all over and grows and bears fruit. Jesus LEADS!
- You can add a scoop of the additional ingredients, if you like. And now hold a bag for your friend. Let's thank Jesus for this food and for His forgiveness. Lead a snack prayer.

Before They Go

SAY: Getting mixed up with sin is bad, but we are all sinful. This mixed-up snack mix looked and tasted pretty good, but the greatest good is that Jesus forgives us. **SAY**: GATHER 'ROUND! (Point up and circle hand.) **JESUS FORGIVES! KIDS AND LEADERS:** (Point up.) **JESUS FORGIVES,** (Circle hand.) **NOW AND FOREVER!**

Games

Feed the Pigs

You Need

- 4 large pieces of cardboard, decorated as a pig's face with a hole cut for the mouth
- 12 beanbags (3 per team)
- 8 cones
- Paper and pens

Get Ready

Using large sheets of cardboard, make a pig's face on each piece. Cut a hole (6–8 inches in diameter) as the mouth of the pig (holes can be larger or smaller, depending of the age of the students). Place pig faces on one side of the playing area and set the cones four feet away. Put three beanbags by each cone. Another ten feet back, place another row of cones for the kids to line up behind.

Here We Go

SAY: Howdy, all! Let's get started here at Bales of Fun Games! In our parable today, Jesus tells a story about a young man who disrespects his family, spends all his inheritance, and finds himself feeding animals as a job. What animal did he feed? (Pigs) Now, while being a pig farmer today is not a bad job, in Jesus' day, feeding the pigs was saved for the lowest servants. At the end of the story, the father forgave the son. Jesus forgives us all our sins too.

Divide the kids into four teams and have each team line up behind the first row of cones.

SAY: When I say "Go!" the first person in line will race up to the next cone and toss three pieces of "food" to feed the pig. Then you run and pick up your beanbags, place them back at the cone and race back to the end of the line. Then the next person can go.

This is a quick and easy game that can be played multiple times. Depending on the abilities of the group, feel free to lengthen or shorten the throwing distance. To slow the pace of the activity and make the goal to aim and not worry about speed, after each round, together as a group count up the total of how many pieces of food all four pigs "ate." After several rounds, when you are finished, **SAY: Does Jesus forgive us when we talk back to our parents?** (Yes) **Does Jesus**

forgive us when we are mean to our friends? (Yes) **Is there anything we can do where Jesus won't forgive us?** (No) Jesus died on the cross so that He could take on all our sin and rose again so that we could have eternal life with Him. And, He also helps us ask for forgiveness from those we hurt, obey our parents, and be kind to our friends. Let's say it together. **SAY: GATHER 'ROUND!** (Point up and circle hand.) **JESUS FORGIVES! KIDS AND LEADERS:** (Point up.) **JESUS FORGIVES,** (Circle hand.) **NOW AND FOREVER!**

Fun in the Play Yard

If your Games time is in a play yard, consider using activities from the Learning Area too. Father, May I? is a possibility.

Or play Pig Out! if you did not do so in Lesson 2. In advance, set up a cone for each relay group to stand behind. About twenty feet away from the cones, set up a table.

Explain that each Team will stand behind a cone and pretend to be pigs. A Leader will pretend to be a farmer and call the first person in line to come for dinner. That child will race down to the table. Designate a Team Leader or volunteer to place a dish of Jell-o out for each child. Keeping their hands behind their backs, the children (pigs) must eat some of the Jell-o and race back to the cone. After everyone has had a turn, **SAY: Even in our lowest moments, Jesus offers us forgiveness and His love! He reaches out to save us from our sinful mess.**

Closing

🕐 **about 20 minutes**

Closing Puppet Skit

You need: *Polly the Pig Puppet*, Puppet Script, *Lesson 4 Little Sprouts Early Childhood Leaflet*, *Lesson 4 My Shepherd Collectible*, and children's take-home items

Seat the children on the floor or carpet squares. **SING:** "My Shepherd" (*Leader CD* Track 17) or "Always and Forever, No Matter What!" (*Leader CD* Track 1). Bring out the *Polly the Pig Puppet* to talk about how there is rejoicing when we say we're sorry for our sins and when we start following our Good Shepherd again. He is always forgiving. Use the Puppet Script from the *Leader CD*.

After the skit, close with this echo prayer: **Dear Jesus, / thank You for being with us / at Barnyard Roundup today. / Help us to remember / that You forgive us now / and forever. / Help us follow You and stay by You always. / Amen.**

SAY: Let's meet again at *Barnyard Roundup*! Next time, we'll hear how Jesus did something amazing so that we would be with Him forever. **SAY:** GATHER 'ROUND! (Point up and circle hand.) **JESUS FORGIVES! KIDS AND LEADERS:** (Point up.) **JESUS FORGIVES,** (Circle hand.) **NOW AND FOREVER! Now let's do it again in a whisper voice.** (Repeat Take-Home Point.) **Now let's do it in our loudest voice.** (Repeat Take-Home Point.)

Show a lesson leaflet. **SAY: Please take this home and ask your Mom or Dad to read it. There is something special on the front and back page for your family to do together.**

Thank your Helpers. Send home *Lesson 4 Little Sprouts Early Childhood Leaflet*, *Lesson 4 My Shepherd Collectible*, and other take-home items. As you say good-bye to children at sign-out time, remind parents to read the leaflet at home.

Looking Ahead

Pray for your students and Helpers.

Restock or prepare Learning Area with Lesson 5 materials.

Lay out *Poster Fun* from *Little Sprouts Early Childhood Leaflets* for the next lesson's transition activity.

Prepare the Storytelling materials.

Review the next lesson's plans. Ask your team members what adjustments might improve the schedule or activities.

Lesson 5
Roundup Leader Devotion
Bible Story: **Jesus Appears to Mary in the Garden**
                John 20:1–18

Bible Memory Verse:
"I shall dwell in the house of the Lord forever." Psalm 23:6

Read John 20:1–18 and
Think on These Things:

This Bible account brings us full circle. In Lesson 1, Jesus explains that the Good Shepherd knows His sheep and calls them by name. They recognize and follow Him. In this lesson, we see these actions again.

John 20:1–10 John tells about the actions of Mary, who, when she saw that the stone was removed from the tomb, left the others, ran to tell Jesus' disciples, and returned to the tomb with Peter and John.

John 20:11–18 When they left, Mary stayed. When she looked in the tomb, she saw two angels in white. Turning toward the garden, she saw Jesus but did not recognize Him.

Jesus changed that simply by speaking her name. "Mary," Jesus said, and she responded immediately, "Rabboni." That word, translated "teacher," shows deep respect. The word of Jesus rolled opened the door of recognition. She knew His voice. By faith and at His Word, she recognized her Lord Jesus, our Good Shepherd.

And what did Jesus do next? He sent her out to share the good news. Her witness? "I have seen the Lord," she said as she told the disciples the words of Jesus.

So Jesus is present with us today. He calls us personally by our name. By faith, we know His voice. It is the voice of our risen Savior. We follow Him.

Take-Home Point:
Jesus is our Savior, now and forever!

Jesus, the Good Shepherd of the sheep, is our Savior, now and forever. Without a Savior, we would remain in our sins. We are defenseless against our enemies of sin, death, and Satan. But Jesus knows our names and calls us to be His own, now and forever. He defends and protects us from our enemies, now and forever. He laid down His life to save us. Because Jesus rose and is alive, we will have life, now and forever.

Jesus Gathers Us Together: Through the power of the Holy Spirit, by faith, we know and believe in our Savior, who achieved victory over death for us. Jesus calls us by name and gathers us to Himself, giving us salvation. We marvel at what Jesus has done for us. We joyfully

tell others the Good News that Jesus is our Savior, who overcame sin and death. May God bless our words and service to His dear children at *Barnyard Roundup*!

Prayer: Jesus, thank You for not holding our past and our sin against us. Thank You for forgiving us. Thank You for loving us so much that You willingly died on the cross to save us and rose again to win the victory over our enemies. Because of these things, we can be with You now and forever. Be with us through Your Word and in the Sacraments. Help us share Your love with others so they may know You as their Savior and their Good Shepherd too. In Your name we pray. Amen.

Lesson 5
Jesus Appears to Mary in the Garden

John 20:1–18

Today You Need

Leader and Student Materials (p. 10)

Every Lesson Supplies (p. 11)

Learning Area Supplies: play dough; small rolling pins; biscuit cutters, round cookie cutters, jar lids, or plastic cups; plastic coffee stirrers or unsharpened pencils; a rhythm instrument

Storytelling Supplies: bandage; small sunflower; 4 paper plates with a face drawn on each; a cross; all 5 *Bible Story Posters*

See the Master Supply List on *Leader CD* for complete list for all lessons.

Welcome, *Poster Fun*, and Learning Areas

 20 minutes

Play music from the *Leader CD* in the background. Have Helpers with nametags stationed inside and outside of the entrance to greet and direct families to the welcome table. While helping children with nametags and attendance stickers, ask the parents/caregivers to use the *Sign In & Out Sheet* each day. Have the children put their sheep in the sheep pen to take attendance.

SAY: Hi, I'm (Leader's name). (Child's name), **welcome to Barnyard Roundup! We'll do so many fun activities here on our last day together. We'll learn more about Jesus and His love for us. We'll hear how He is with us, providing for us and protecting us. You can go to the *Poster Fun* table. The Helpers will give you the posters and directions.**

Poster Fun Helpers give out posters and directions. Make sure first and last names are printed on the posters. Remind parents to leave the posters on the table before moving to the next activity. Helpers gather posters and get them ready to be taken home at the end of this lesson.

Poster Fun for Parents and Kids

You need: your child's *Poster Fun*, blue crayon, and *Resurrected Jesus Sticker*

Parents: Make sure you have the same *Poster Fun* your child used last time. Look at the picture on the front with your child. **SAY: This picture reminds me of the fun you have been having at *Barnyard Roundup*. Do you see the little pictures at the bottom? What did these stories teach you about Jesus?** Let your child share. Repeat the Take-Home Points, if possible.

Turn the poster over to the back page. Have your child repeat the Lesson 5 Bible Memory Verse after you. Point to the last shepherd staff icon. **SAY: Shepherds use this to keep sheep from going away. They keep the sheep near them. Jesus gathers us together. He will lead us to heaven to be with Him forever! Color the staff blue.**

Open *Poster Fun* and point to the Lesson 5 picture. **SAY: Do you see the crosses?** Help your child point to the crosses. **We know that Jesus died on the cross to take our sins away. Today, you will learn how this lady** (point to Mary) **saw Jesus after He came alive again on the first Easter.** Give your child the *Resurrected Jesus Sticker*. **SAY: Let's put this sticker of Jesus here for Mary to see. Repeat after me: JESUS IS OUR SAVIOR, NOW AND FOREVER.**

Leave the leaflet on the table. Take your child to Learning Area 1. Once your child is engaged in the activity, you may quietly leave.

Transition Activities

Learning Area 1: Make It
Play dough Feelings

Goal: The children will create play-dough faces showing the different emotions in the Bible story: sadness, surprise, joy.

You need: play dough; small rolling pins; biscuit cutters, round cookie cutters, jar lids, or plastic cups; plastic coffee stirrers or unsharpened pencils

Invite children to sit and play with the dough. Demonstrate rolling out or patting the play dough and cutting circle shapes. Assist as needed. If you don't have enough dough for each child to make three faces, have them reshape their dough each time.

SAY: In our Bible story, we are going to hear about when Jesus died on the cross to take our sins away and then came alive again on Easter. His friends had a lot of different feelings that day. First, they were sad. Can you make a sad face? Children cut out a circle and use the coffee stirrer to create a sad face.

SAY: Next, Jesus' friends were surprised. Show me what your face would look like if you were surprised. Encourage the children to open their eyes wide and make their mouth into an O shape. **Let's see if we can make a surprised face with our play dough.** Children cut out another circle and make big eyes and an O-shaped mouth.

SAY: At the end of our story, a lady named Mary saw that Jesus was alive. She was so happy. Now let's make happy faces. Children cut out another circle and make a happy face. They may want to use their coffee stirrer or roll a small piece of play dough like a snake to form a mouth that can curve up into a smile.

Learning Area Options:

Bible Story Coloring Pages: Use the lesson's Coloring Page as a Learning Area for a quiet and calm coloring station. Helpers can encourage the children to identify objects and people on the Coloring Page. Then they can tell the children that they will be hearing this Bible story a little later.

Learning Area 2: Imagine It
Who Knows My Name?

Goal: The children will guess who is saying their name.

You need: nothing

At this last session, children may know one another's names. If not, review everyone's name in the group.

SAY: In our story, a lady named Mary is crying. She doesn't know Jesus is alive. Then Jesus says her name and she knows it's Him by the sound of His voice. We learned that Jesus, the Good Shepherd, knows the names of us, His sheep, and we know His voice. Now let's see how well we know one another's voices.

Choose a child to come to the front of the group and be "it." The child who is "it" will have his or her back to the others and will cover his or her eyes with his or her hands. **SAY: The rest of us must be very, very quiet. I will point to one of you, and you need to say** (the child)**'s name.** (The child)**, try to guess who said your name.** Indicate to the children to be quiet. Point to a child to say "it's" name. To "it," **SAY: Do you know who said your name?** After "it" guesses, let him or her know if the guess was correct. If not, try again. Continue until all children have had a turn to listen and guess. Conclude with a song.

SING (to the tune of the "Farmer in the Dell"):

> Jesus knows my name. Jesus knows my name,
> He died and rose again. Jesus knows my name.

Learning Area 3: Act It Out
Listen and Move

Goal: The children will listen to a rhythm and move according to the speed of the beat.

You need: a rhythm instrument (e.g., tambourine, bell, triangle, rhythm sticks or 2 blocks to hit together)

SAY: In the Bible story, Jesus' friends went to the tomb. They were very sad. Do you think they walked or ran? (Accept answers.) **How would you walk if you were sad?** Children demonstrate a slow walk.

SAY: When they got to the tomb, they looked inside. They had to stoop to look into the tomb. Demonstrate stooping. **Later, the friends were very excited when they saw that Jesus was alive. What do you think they did?** (Ran to tell others) Demonstrate.

SAY: I am going to play this instrument in three different ways. If I play it slowly, I want you to walk in place and pretend you are sad. Demonstrate a slow, steady rhythm. **If I do just one short sound, you are to stoop down and then stand back up.** Demonstrate one short sound. **If I play the instrument quickly, I want you to run in place and pretend you're excited.** Demonstrate a quick, steady rhythm.

Play the instrument the three different ways, first in sequence from walking to stooping to jogging in place, then mix them up. Continue as interest allows.

Opening

🕐 **20 minutes**

You need: altar, Lyrics Sheets, *Leader CD*, Puppet Scripts and prop, *Polly the Pig Puppet*, bell, Bible

Ring the bell to get everyone's attention. **SING** (to the tune of "The Farmer in the Dell"):

> It's Bible story time. It's Bible story time.
> We're going to hear how Jesus saves.
> It's Bible story time!

Repeat as needed, encouraging the children to sing along as they move toward the altar area and are seated.

SAY: I am so happy to see you again at our *Barnyard Roundup*. **We have had such a great time learning about God and His love. Last time, we learned that Jesus forgives. Jesus told a story about a man who forgave his son. What did the son do?** (Accept answers about how he went away, spent his money, and came back.) **We found out that Jesus told stories to help people learn about God's love. But then Jesus did something to *show* God's love and forgiveness. He died on the cross to take our sins away.** Point to the altar cross. **In the Bible, we hear that Good News.** Hold up the Bible. **Because Jesus took our sins away, we will live forever with God in heaven!**

Show the children how to fold their hands. **SAY: In the name of the Father and of the Son and of the Holy Spirit. Amen. We say those words to remember that God is with us. Now I am going to light the candle to remind us that Jesus is the Light. The sun shines every day, and Jesus shines on us every day!** Light the candle.

SING: "I Am Jesus' Little Lamb" (*Leader CD* Track 15) or "All Together Come and Gather" (*Leader CD* Track 2).

Teach the Take-Home Point

SAY: What do sheep need to be saved from? What could harm them? (Wild animals, rough terrain like cliffs or holes, bad weather, thieves) **Jesus is our Good Shepherd. He takes care of our biggest need— protecting us from our enemies: sin, death, and the devil. Jesus saves us, so He is called our Savior.**

SAY: GATHER 'ROUND! (Point up and circle hand.) **JESUS IS OUR SAVIOR! KIDS AND LEADERS:** (Point up.) **JESUS IS OUR SAVIOR,** (Circle hand.) **NOW AND FOREVER! Now let's do it again in a whisper voice.** Repeat Take-Home Point. **Now let's do it in our loudest voice.** Repeat Take-Home Point.

Pray

Have the children sit down. **SAY: Now let's talk to God by praying.** Invite the children to fold their hands, bow their heads, and repeat each phrase of the prayer after you. Pause after each forward slash mark (/).

SAY: Dear Father, / You are so good to us. / Thank You / for sending Jesus / to be our Savior. / We can't wait / to live with You forever. / We love You! / Amen.

Opening Puppet Skit

You need: *Polly the Pig Puppet*, Puppet Script (*Leader CD*), bandage, sunflower (small artificial or paper flower)

The farmer saves Polly from a tornado.

After the skit, **SAY: Wow! Polly could have really been hurt! The farmer could have been hurt too, but he still cared enough to go out and save Polly. Now let's hear about someone who saved *us*!**

Bible Storytelling

🕐 20 minutes

You need: 4 paper plates with a face drawn on each (one with an angry face drawn on it, one with a sad face, one with a surprised face, and one with a happy face); a cross

SAY: Jesus had helped many people. Some were sick, and He made them well. Some were hungry, and He fed them. All of them needed to hear about God's love, and Jesus told them. They were so happy to hear God's Word! Hold up the happy-face plate.

Hold up the angry-face plate. **SAY: But some people did not like what Jesus was saying. So those people did something very sad.** Hold up the sad-face plate. **They put Jesus on the cross, and He died.** Hold up the cross. **Jesus' friends were very sad.** Show the sad-face plate again. **After Jesus died, His friends took Him down from the cross and buried Him in a cave called a tomb. A huge stone was rolled in front of the tomb.**

SAY: Two days later, a friend of Jesus' named Mary went to the tomb. When she got there, she was surprised! Show the surprised-face plate. **The stone was rolled away from the tomb. She looked inside and saw that Jesus was gone! So she ran to tell Jesus' other friends.** Pat your hands on your legs really fast to make a running sound. Demonstrate patting hands on legs and encourage the children to join in. **Mary told Jesus' other friends, "Jesus is not in the tomb; someone must have taken Him!"**

SAY: Now Peter and John ran. Pat legs again to make a running sound. **John got there first and stooped down and looked into the tomb. Then Peter came and went into the tomb. They were surprised too!** Hold up surprised-face plate again. **Then Peter and John went home.**

SAY: But Mary stayed by the tomb. She was crying. Show the sad-face plate. **She heard a man behind her. He said, "Woman, why are you crying?"**

Mary said, "If you have taken away Jesus, please tell me where He is."

SAY: Then the man said her name, "Mary." It was Jesus! Hold up the surprised-face plate. **Mary said, "Rabboni!" That is a word that means "teacher." Jesus really was alive! It was really Him! Mary recognized His voice.**

Jesus told Mary to go and tell His friends that He was alive. So Mary ran back to Jesus' friends. Pat hands on legs. **She said, "I have seen Jesus! He really is alive!"** Show the happy-face plate.

Show the cross. **Jesus died on the cross to take away our sins. Then He came alive again on Easter. Someday we will die, but we will come alive again and live with Jesus forever in heaven. Jesus is our Good Shepherd. He will gather up all His flock and bring us all to be with Him now and forever.**

Let's say our Take-Home Point.

SAY: GATHER 'ROUND! (Point up and circle hand.) **JESUS IS OUR SAVIOR! KIDS AND LEADERS:** (Point up.) **JESUS IS OUR SAVIOR,** (Circle hand.) **NOW AND FOREVER!**

Ring the bell and **SAY: It's time to move. Follow your Leaders.**

Rotation Sites

🕐 **1 hour**

Early Childhood Teams get into three Rotation Groups. Each Rotation Group moves to their assigned Rotation Site. When it is time to move to a different Rotation Site, ring a bell three times.

Rotation 1: Bible Story Application

🕐 **About 20 minutes**

Review

You need: *Lesson 5 Little Sprouts Early Childhood Leaflet* and stickers, crayons (including multiple crayons of the same color)

Give *Lesson 5 Little Sprouts Early Childhood Leaflets* to small-group Leaders. Sit at tables or on carpet squares in a circle on the floor. Make sure each child's name gets on his or her leaflet. As you pass out each one, **SAY: This is for Jesus' little lamb** (name of child). When all the leaflets are distributed, **SAY: You are one of His precious children. You will get to live with Him in heaven forever! Let's review why.**

SAY: Look at the picture on the front of your leaflet. Do you see the city? Children point to the city. **On Good Friday, people led Jesus outside of that city and to a cross. What happened on the cross?** (Jesus died on the cross to save us by taking our sins away.) **Point to where they buried Jesus' body.** Children point to the tomb. **Is Jesus in the tomb?** (No, He is alive!) **Point to Mary.** Children point to Mary. **What is she doing?** Discuss. **She is so surprised and happy to see Jesus. Let's look inside the leaflet and see what makes us happy.**

Leaflet Activity

Pass out the stickers for Lesson 5. **SAY: Our stickers are all the same. What do you see on the stickers?** (A heart with a cross on it.) **What does a heart remind you of?** (Love) **God loved us so much that He sent Jesus to die on the cross to save us from our sins. So the heart and the cross belong together.**

SAY: When I look at this picture, I smile. It reminds me of how wonderful it will be in heaven with Jesus. Point to the sun. Children point to the sun. **What color should we make the sun?** (Yellow) As the children color, **SAY: Does the sun come up every day?** (Yes) **Always?** (Always) **You know what else happens each day? Jesus loves us every day! Will He always love us?** (Always!)

SAY: Point to the water. What color should we make the water? (Blue) As the children color, **SAY: Water reminds**

me that Jesus washes my sins away. Let's put a sticker by the water. Children add a sticker by the water.

SAY: Point to the grass. Children point to the grass. **What color should we make the grass?** (Green.) As children color the grass, **SAY: Do you remember how a good shepherd leads his sheep to eat the good grass? That reminds me that God will always provide for me and give me everything I need, now and forever. Jesus leads us to heaven, where we will never be hungry.**

SAY: Point to the wheat, the plants with seeds. Children point to the wheat. **These plants have grown up strong and made new seeds. That reminds me of how God helps us listen to His Word, grow in our faith, and share His love with others. Put a sticker by these plants.** Children add the sticker by the wheat.

SAY: I see some beautiful sunflowers. Point to them. Children point to the sunflowers. **We will make these sunflowers the same color as the sun.** Children color the sunflowers yellow. As they color, **SAY: Remember in our story when Mary was crying? In the Bible, God tells us that there won't be any crying in heaven. These sunflowers make me feel happy, just like when I remember that Jesus came alive again on Easter.**

SAY: I see a man. Who is it? (Jesus) **Our sin separates us from God. Because of sin, we can't be with Him. But because Jesus died on the cross and rose from the dead, we can be with God. Draw yourself next to Jesus.** Allow time for children to draw themselves walking next to Jesus. **Let's put a sticker here to remind us that because Jesus died on the cross to save us, we will live with Him forever in heaven. Jesus has called us to Himself, by name. He leads us to heaven!** Allow children to finish coloring the picture.

SAY: GATHER 'ROUND! (Point up and circle hand.) **JESUS IS OUR SAVIOR! KIDS AND LEADERS:** (Point up.) **JESUS IS OUR SAVIOR,** (Circle hand.) **NOW AND FOREVER!**

Sing: "The Baa, Baa Song" (*Leader CD* Track 18) or "Love In a Box" (*Leader CD* Track 16).

Rotation 2: Bible Challenge

🕐 **About 20 minutes**

The Bible Memory Song

You need: Bible with the Bible Memory Verse marked, *Bible Memory Songs Sign Chart, Leader CD,* and a CD player

SAY: Our Bible Memory Verse is "I shall dwell in the house of the LORD forever," Psalm 23:6. Those words are from God's book, the Bible. Let's sing this Bible Memory Verse together. Play *Leader CD* Track 13. Add the motions as shown on the *Bible Memory Songs Sign Chart.*

Story Review

You need: all 5 *Bible Story Posters*

Hold all the Bible Story Posters on your lap, but do not show them. **SAY: I have some posters here from all our VBS Bible stories that we have learned about. I am going to tell you something about the poster, and then I want you to tell me what you think is on the poster.**

SAY: The first poster is about Jesus being our Good Shepherd. Who can tell me something they think will be on the poster? Accept answers. If the children can't think of anything, give hints, such as, "This is who the shepherd takes care of," "This is something green that sheep like to eat," "This is something wet that sheep like to drink," or "This is something a shepherd carries when he is walking." When the children can't think of anything else that might be on the poster, show it to them and point out how many things they guessed correctly.

Review the Take-Home Point. **SAY: GATHER 'ROUND!** (Point up and circle hand.) **JESUS CARES! KIDS AND LEADERS:** (Point up.) **JESUS CARES,** (Circle hand.) **NOW AND FOREVER!**

SAY: The second poster is about when Jesus fed 5,000 people. Who can tell me something they think will be on the poster? Accept answers. If the children can't think of anything, give hints, such as, "This is what the people ate," "This is where the people sat," "This is what the bread was in," or "This is someone who shared his lunch." When the children can't think of anything else that might be on the poster, show it to them and point out how many things they guessed correctly.

SAY: GATHER 'ROUND! (Point up and circle hand.) **JESUS PROVIDES! KIDS AND LEADERS:** (Point up.) **JESUS PROVIDES,** (Circle hand.) **NOW AND FOREVER!**

SAY: The third poster shows the story Jesus told about the farmer who was planting seeds. Who can tell me something they think will be on the poster? Accept answers. If the children can't think of anything, give hints, such as, "This is something that likes to eat seeds," "This is something that holds the seeds," or "This is something on top of healthy plants." When the children can't think of anything else that might be on the poster, show it to them and point out how many things they guessed correctly.

SAY: GATHER 'ROUND! (Point up and circle hand.) **JESUS LEADS! KIDS AND LEADERS:** (Point up.) **JESUS LEADS,** (Circle hand.) **NOW AND FOREVER!**

SAY: The fourth poster is the one about the loving father. Who can tell me something they think will be on the poster? Accept answers. If the children can't think of anything, give hints, such as, "This is what the son was wearing after he spent all his money," "How did the other brother feel?" or "This is what the father did when the son came back." When the children can't think of anything else that might be on the poster, show it to them and point out how many things they guessed correctly.

SAY: GATHER 'ROUND! (Point up and circle hand.) **JESUS FORGIVES! KIDS AND LEADERS:** (Point up.) **JESUS FORGIVES,** (Circle hand.) **NOW AND FOREVER!**

SAY: This is our poster from today's story. Who remembers what was on the poster? Accept answers. If the children can't think of anything, give hints, such as, "This is where they placed Jesus' body" or "This is who was in front of the tomb," "This is who is no longer in the tomb." When the children can't think of anything else that might be on the poster, show it to them and point out how many things they guessed correctly.

Conclude with another Take-Home Point activity. **SAY: GATHER 'ROUND!** (Point up and circle hand.) **JESUS IS OUR SAVIOR! KIDS AND LEADERS:** (Point up.) **JESUS IS OUR SAVIOR,** (Circle hand.) **NOW AND FOREVER!**

Rotation 3: Crafts

🕐 **20 minutes**

My Savior Kite

You Need

- *My Savior Kite*, 1 per person
- Markers
- Finished sample craft

Make It!

Gather needed materials. Leaders put the child's name on the back of the craft. Show the children the supplies and markers. Help and encourage the children as needed.

Give children ample workspace on a flat surface, even on the floor, if necessary. Children use the markers to color the kite. Leaders attach the kite string for flying it.

Putting It All Together

SAY: We have learned a lot about Jesus, our Good Shepherd. We learned that Jesus cares, provides, leads, forgives, and is our Savior. Without Jesus' help, we would remain in our sins. But Jesus knows our names and calls us to be His own. He defends and protects us against sin, death, and the devil. He laid down His life to save us. Because Jesus rose and is alive, we can have life in heaven.

After Mary learned Jesus was alive, she ran to tell others the Good News. Jesus also gives us His Good News to share! Let's make a kite that has pictures of the Easter story. When you fly it, use those pictures to share the Good News with others: Jesus is our Savior, now and forever!

On the kite, identify the crosses where Jesus died to pay for our sins and the empty tomb that shows Jesus rose from the dead. The sun reminds us that Jesus is the Son of God and our Savior, who rose on Easter morning. As sure as the sun will rise every morning, we can be sure of Jesus' love. The Greek letters Alpha and Omega remind us that our God is the beginning and the end, who is with us now and forever! The palm branches recall when Jesus rode a donkey into Jerusalem on Palm Sunday and the people shouted, "Blessed is He who comes in the name of the Lord!" (Matthew 21:9).

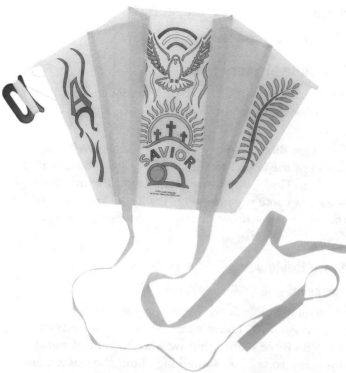

SAY: GATHER 'ROUND! (Point up and circle hand.) JESUS IS OUR SAVIOR! **KIDS AND LEADERS:** (Point up.) JESUS IS OUR SAVIOR, (Circle hand.) NOW AND FOREVER!

Ask your VBS Director when you or someone else can demonstrate to the children how to fly a kite. Also allow the children to practice. Opportunities might include time during Games or after your VBS session concludes. Even if the weather is not ideal, children can practice how to hold the kite as they run to launch it.

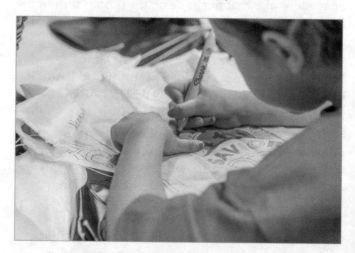

Snack

20 minutes

Let Love Show

You Need

- A plate for each child
- A wooden craft stick for each child
- Two pieces of sandwich bread for each child
- Strawberry or raspberry jam
- Sun butter (made from sunflower seeds; peanut and tree-nut free)
- Heart-shaped cookie cutters
- Hand sanitizer & napkins
- Cups & water

Advance Preparation

Before the session, put items listed above on each Team's table. Put one tablespoon of sun butter and a craft stick on each plate.

When Kids Arrive

Take the children to the restroom. Have them wash their hands. Have them sit in their places.

SAY: We have been learning verses from Psalm 23. Let's say today's verse: "I will dwell in the house of the LORD forever," Psalm 23:6. Because of sin, we might doubt Jesus is always with us when we can't see Him. Today's Bible story is about someone who saw Jesus after He rose from the dead! Can you imagine how wonderful that would be? Even though we can't see Jesus, we can be certain He is with us because He promises never to leave us. Jesus is our Savior, now and forever!

Making the Snack

Demonstrate step by step as you explain how to make the snack:

- Start with two pieces of bread. Use a craft stick to spread jam on one piece. The red jam reminds us of the blood Jesus shed when He died on the cross to pay for our sins.
- Next, spread sun butter on the other piece of bread. Sun butter is made from sunflower seeds. God plants the seed of faith in our heart. We produce a harvest in our acts of service and words of love.

- If we close the sandwich now, we wouldn't be able to see what's inside. Likewise, we can't see Jesus, but we can see everything He provides. Others see Jesus in *us* by the fruits of our faith in the love and care we show them.
- Let's use a heart-shaped cookie cutter to cut a heart in the middle of the piece of bread with sun butter.
- Finally, put your sandwich together. You can see the red jam inside of the sandwich through the heart-shaped cut-out! Show the children how to set the heart back inside the sandwich. **Our snack shows that even if we can't see Jesus, we "see" and experience His goodness and mercy. Jesus works through us to share His love with others through what we do and say.**

Lead a snack prayer and eat.

Before They Go

SAY: Our snack reminds us that Jesus is our Savior. Without Jesus, our Savior, we would be stuck in our sin. Because we know Jesus died and rose again for us, we share the Good News with others. Share the Take-Home Point. **SAY: GATHER 'ROUND!** (Point up and circle hand.) **JESUS IS OUR SAVIOR! KIDS AND LEADERS:** (Point up.) **JESUS IS OUR SAVIOR,** (Circle hand.) **NOW AND FOREVER!**

Games

🕐 20 minutes

Gather the Eggs

You Need

- 4 dozen plastic eggs
  (1 dozen of the same color per team)
- 4 empty egg cartons
- 4 farmer hats

Get Ready

In a large playing area, scatter and/or hide all the eggs.

For younger kids, it might be helpful to put a color marking on each of the cartons, so they remember what color eggs they are looking for. Another adaptation for younger players would be to scatter the eggs instead of hiding them.

Here We Go

SAY: Well, farmers, it's our last time at Bales of Fun Games! Today, we are talking about a beautiful Bible story where Jesus, right after He has risen from the grave, calls Mary by name and calls her as His own. We are all His own and He gathers us to Himself. Just as Jesus gathers us all together, we need to gather the eggs that have been laid all over the place.

Before the game starts, divide the kids into four teams. Each Team needs to pick one person to be the farmer and decide what farm animal the rest of the team will be. Make sure the Teams don't share with other Teams what animals they are, and make sure each Team chooses a different animal. Assist the children as necessary; assign the farmer and animal name, if desired.

Leaders designate each Team with one color egg and give an egg carton and hat to each farmer.

SAY: When I say "Go!" all the animals run loose to find their color of eggs. But animals can't pick up eggs; only the farmer can. And animals can't talk; they can only make their own animal noise. The farmers must listen carefully to find their animals, who are hopefully showing their farmer all twelve of their Team's eggs. Once a farmer has filled a carton, yell, "Gather 'round, the eggs are found!" The first Team to find all twelve eggs of their color wins.

You will probably want to play this game again. Quickly scatter the eggs in the playing area and pick a new farmer. You could also challenge the Teams to make no noise, but only actions to notify their farmer. When finished, have the students sit together. **ASK, How are we gathered into the family of God?** (Through our Baptism) **God calls each and every one of us to be His son or daughter. As children of God, what good gifts to we receive?** (God's love, forgiveness, eternal life) **What awesome news! SAY: GATHER 'ROUND!** (Point up and circle hand.) **JESUS IS OUR SAVIOR! KIDS AND LEADERS:** (Point up.) **JESUS IS OUR SAVIOR,** (Circle hand.) **NOW AND FOREVER!**

Fun in the Play Yard

If your Games time is in a play yard, consider using activities from the Learning Area too. Listen and Move is a possibility.

Or play a simplified version of Gather the Eggs. Use the same materials, but no farmer hats. In advance, hide lots of plastic eggs or small, soft balls or tennis balls around the playing area.

Divide the children into pairs or groups of three, depending on the size of your class. Let the children work together to collect as many eggs as they can in a certain time period, to collect all the eggs of a certain color, or to just fill up their carton. Allow talking, and let each child pretend to be a farmer.

Closing

🕐 **about 15 minutes**

Closing Puppet Skit

You need: *Polly the Pig Puppet*, Puppet Script and prop, *Lesson 5 Little Sprouts Early Childhood Leaflet, Lesson 5 My Shepherd Collectible*, and children's take-home items

Seat the children on the floor or carpet squares. **SING:** "I Shall Dwell in the House of the Lord Forever" (*Leader CD* Track 4) or "He Is Risen" (*Leader CD* Track 3).

Bring out the *Polly the Pig Puppet* to talk about how great a feeling it is that Jesus is our Savior, now and forever. Use the Puppet Script from the *Leader CD*.

After the skit, close with this echo prayer:

Dear Jesus, / thank You for being with us / at *Barnyard Roundup*. / Help us to remember / that You are our Savior /now and forever. / Keep us safe as we go home now. / And lead us to our home in heaven, / where we will be with You forever. /Amen.

Show a lesson leaflet. **SAY: Please take this home and ask your Mom or Dad to read it. There is something special on it for your family to do together.**

SAY: *Barnyard Roundup* **is over, and we've had fun together and learned so much about Jesus, our Savior. You can learn more about Jesus and His love**

at church and at Sunday School. (If your church has a preschool, mention it here as well.)

SAY: Let's say thank you to all of our Helpers by clapping. Enjoy the rest of your summer as you share the Good News that Jesus is your Good Shepherd, who provides for you and protects you, now and always.

Thank your Helpers. Send home *Lesson 5 Little Sprouts Early Childhood Leaflet, Lesson 5 My Shepherd Collectible,* and other take-home items. As you say good-bye to children at sign-out time, remind parents to read the leaflet at home and thank them for bringing their child to VBS.

Looking Ahead

Pray for your students and their families.

Thank your Helpers, and thank God for blessing your VBS.

Check with your Director for a list of things to do at the conclusion of VBS.

Restore your area to its pre-VBS condition. Return any borrowed items.

Fill out your evaluation online at cph.org/vbsfeedback.

We Want Your Feedback

We want to hear from you. Let us know what we did right, and help us learn where we can improve. Save time and postage by going online to www.cph.org/VBSfeedback. Please forward this link to all of your volunteers to ensure more comprehensive feedback. Online responses help us compile the results more efficiently and allow us to more quickly review your responses. You will find surveys for both the Director and the Volunteers at the link below. Thank you for your participation. Your feedback is valuable in helping us provide a VBS with Purpose!

www.cph.org/VBSfeedback

Volunteer Survey
Vacation Bible School

SAVE A STAMP and use the online form at cph.org/VBSfeedback

1. Name _____
   Address _____
   State/Province _____ ZIP/Postal Code _____

   Denomination _____

   State/Province _____ ZIP/Postal Code _____

   Ministry Staff   ○ Pastor   ○ DCE   ○ Congregation Member   ○ Other

   w many years of VBS leadership experience do you have?
   –5   ○ 6–10   ○ 11–20   ○ 21+

   ○ **Site leader at:**   or   ○ **Helper at:**
   sing   ○ Storytelling   ○ Bible Challenge   ○ Crafts   ○ Music
   dy   ○ Games   ○ Preschool   ○ Adult Bible Study   ○ Snacks
   pecify) _____

   Publishing House resources did you use in your role at VBS? (check all that apply)
   g Guide & DVD   ○ Music Leader Guide & CD   ○ Bible Challenge Guide & CD
   e & CD   ○ Elementary Leaflets   ○ Game Guide
            ○ Snack Guide   ○ Youth/Adult Bible Study
   e & CD   ○ Preschool Leaflets   ○ Other _____

   n of the resources you used?
   y to use   ○ Helpful but difficult to use
   not very helpful   ○ Difficult to use and not very helpful
   if _____

   n of the Volunteer Training site?
   ○ Helpful but needs more
   ○ Didn't know about it
   rces would help you on this site? _____

   es outside of the lesson plans?
   , please specify: _____

   these resources more helpful? _____

Director Survey
Vacation Bible School

SAVE A STAMP and use the online form at cph.org/VBSfeedback

1. Name _____
   Address _____
   City _____ State/Province _____ ZIP/Postal Code _____
   Email _____

2. Church Name _____ Denomination _____
   Church Address _____
   City _____ State/Province _____ ZIP/Postal Code _____
   Email _____

3. I am a . . . ○ Pastor   ○ DCE   ○ Children's Ministry Director   ○ Volunteer Director   ○ Other
   ○ Male   ○ Female   ○ 20–30   ○ 31–40   ○ 41–55   ○ 56+

4. What date(s) did you host VBS? ____ /_____ /____
   In what month did you decide which VBS program to use? _____

5. What is the format of your VBS?   ○ 1 week, mornings   ○ 1 week, evenings   ○ 1 week, full day
   ○ Backyard camp   ○ Weekend   ○ One-day   ○ Other _____

6. How many children did you host at your VBS?
   ○ 0–24   ○ 25–49   ○ 50–99   ○ 100–199   ○ 200–499   ○ 500–999   ○ 1000+
   This was (circle one)   **greater than**   **less than**   last year by about this many: _____

7. How many children came from outside your church membership/regular attendees?
   ○ 0–24   ○ 25–49   ○ 50–99   ○ 100–199   ○ 200–499   ○ 500–999   ○ 1000+

8. How many volunteers did you have at your VBS?
   ○ 0–9   ○ 10–19   ○ 20–49   ○ 50–99   ○ 100–249   ○ 250+

9. What are the age ranges of the students you serve (lowest age to highest age)?
   preschool: ages ____ to ____   **elementary:** ages ____ to ____
   youth: ages ____ to ____ (youth VBS, not volunteers)   **adults:** ages ____ to ____ (adult VBS, not volunteers)

10. How did teens participate in your VBS? (Check all that apply.)
    ○ Students   ○ Team (small-group) leaders   ○ Site leaders   ○ Site assistants   ○ Other _____

11. Please share with us your favorite *Barnyard Roundup* memory or special comments you received from attendees.
    _____
    _____
    _____
    _____
    _____